ZYZZYVA

Volume XXXV, Number 1

Spring/Summer 2019

A SAN FRANCISCO JOURNAL OF ARTS AND LETTERS

SINCE 1985

ZYZZYVA

EDITOR
Laura Cogan

MANAGING EDITOR
Oscar Villalon

EDITORIAL ASSISTANT
Zack Ravas

SALES & MARKETING
Laura Howard

CONTRIBUTING EDITORS
Andrew Foster Altschul, Sam Barry,
Robin Ekiss, John Freeman, Paul Madonna,
Ismail Muhammad, David L. Ulin

COPY EDITOR
Regan McMahon

INTERNS
Casey Jong, Katie O'Neill

BOARD OF DIRECTORS
Warren Lazarow, *President*
Laura Cogan
Patrick Corman
Jane Gillette
Regis McKenna
Barbara Meacham
Jonathan Schmidt

ORIGINAL DESIGN
Three Steps Ahead

TYPE DESIGN
Text font created specially for
ZYZZYVA by Matthew Butterick

PRODUCTION
Josh Korwin

PRINTER
Versa Press, Inc.

DISTRIBUTION
Publishers Group West

SUBSCRIPTION SERVICES
EBSCO

ARCHIVES
Bancroft Library, UC Berkeley

CONTACT
57 Post St., #604, San Francisco, CA 94104
E contact@zyzzyva.org
W www.zyzzyva.org

SUBSCRIPTION
$42/four issues; $70/eight issues
Student rate: $30/four issues

ZYZZYVA (ISBN 978-1-7329808-0-8) is published in April,
August, and December by ZYZZYVA, Inc., a nonprofit,
tax-exempt corporation. © 2019 ZYZZYVA, Inc.

MIX
Paper from
responsible sources
FSC
www.fsc.org FSC® C005010

**National
Endowment
for the Arts**
arts.gov

ART WORKS.

OUR PAPER STOCK is selected on the basis of its reduced
environmental impact. Text printed on Glatfelter Natures
Antique (30% post-consumer waste). Cover printed on
Kallima Coated Cover C2S. Both papers are FSC® certified.

SPECIAL THANKS

Publication of this issue is made possible in part by the generous support of the National Endowment for the Arts. ZYZZYVA is grateful to The Edward Gorey Charitable Trust, The Phillips Collection, and The Cy Twombly Foundation for permission to reprint the images in this issue.

CONTENTS

VISUAL ART

Edward Gorey, 85, 93 • Diana Guerrero-Maciá, 137–144 • Jordan Kantor, 96
Paul Klee, 31 • Cy Twombly, 109, 111

FRONT & BACK COVERS

Diana Guerrero-Maciá, *The Beautiful Girls no. 4*, 2018, blind embossment and
    collage on archival inkjet print, 17 × 14 inches, courtesy: the artist and Traywick
    Contemporary, Berkeley; photographed by Richard Sprengler

Diana Guerrero-Maciá, *The Beautiful Girls no. 1*, 2018, printed linen and collage
    on archival inkjet print, 17 × 14 inches, courtesy: the artist and Traywick
    Contemporary, Berkeley; photographed by Richard Sprengler

FORTHCOMING

Our next issue publishes in August, closes for ads June 1, 2019.

Zyzzyva.

(ZIZ-zi-va) n. A San Francisco
literary journal; any of various
tropical American weevils of the
genus *Zyzzyva*. The last word in
the Oxford English Dictionary.

"As mythic and wild with
love, possibility, and danger
as the decades it spans;
you'll read *The Light Years*
with your breath held."

—EMMA CLINE, author of *THE GIRLS*

"Darkly comic and told with fire and wisdom,
The Light Years is an iconic American story,
the mad love child of Jack Kerouac, Timothy Leary, and Augusten Burroughs,
Chris Rush's psychedelic life has been truly stranger than fiction."

—ALEXANDRIA MARZANO-LESNEVICH, author of *THE FACT OF A BODY*

NEW THIS SPRING FROM
FARRAR, STRAUS AND GIROUX

START READING
fsgbooks.com

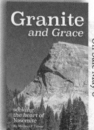

LETTER FROM THE EDITOR

"When power narrows the area of man's concern, poetry reminds him of the richness and diversity of his existence."

—John F. Kennedy

Dear Reader,

Since our first issue in 1985, one of the defining characteristics of this journal has been the curated inclusion of contemporary visual art. While these works make an obviously complimentary counterpoint to the literature we publish, the task of presenting them is not a simple one. We're limited in what we can include by several factors, down to the aspect ratio of these pages. Yet we've persisted in not only including art but also stretching to do more with it (such as when, in Issue No. 92, we added color for the first time), because it is an important part of ZYZZYVA and does so much more than simply look pleasing.

Visual art is an essential element of the conversation we're finding in our community of creators and reporting back to you—our readers—for consideration.

The art and literature we feature often address similar ideas. But just as poetry and prose differ in their ways of making meaning, so does the art. In part this is because the experience of viewing photographs and paintings (the forms we most frequently publish) collapses time in a way that reading cannot.

In this issue we've gathered work from every genre to deliberately consider what art and artists do. The writing here examines art's role in the public square, in a democracy, and in the private life of the individual who comes to art—whether as beholder or creator—always seeking something.

Art often plays the role of provocateur, at once inviting analysis and resisting a final interpretation. In this way, it is not only essential for its own sake but also (sometimes purposefully, other times inadvertently) plays an alchemical role in any democratic society, where citizens are constantly challenged to understand one another—to sacrifice the gratification of the individual's every need to the larger project of living with others. This means working with perspectives we do not fully understand or accept. It means challenging our perceptions.

In our fractured, impatient, and too-often selfish society, we're increasingly in need of conversations that can tolerate ambiguity, that keep space for wonder, for the weird and the unresolved. Art's role is often to complicate, to dwell in uncertainty and complexity, to linger in nuance. But it can also clarify, and evoke essential truths outside the language of argument. Indeed, at times language itself seems fundamentally compromised as a means of communication.

Perhaps we feel the need for art most acutely in times of recidivism, in times of decline, precisely when art seems to excel at impelling us beyond the obvious, beyond degraded norms. Today we need open-ended discussions and spaces for careful consideration. We need, quite desperately, to resist the comforts of simplicity and the lure of conformity.

Spending time with art, and spending time discussing art, has the power not only to enrich our interior lives but also to spark the kind of imagination, empathy, and tolerance for what we do not understand, which serves us well as members of a community.

Issue No. 115 contemplates how we look at art, how art makes meaning, how we sometimes think of our own lives as art, how we seek to be saved (or wrecked) by art, the fatigue and frustration of art tourism, and how the presence of art in public and private arenas unsettles and provokes.

There are also a few pieces here that are not exactly on-theme. But they're excellent; and it's a small sacrifice to include them and in doing so make the whole of the issue that much better.

Yours,

L.

CATHEDRAL:
SOME MARGINALIA ON READING

PAISLEY REKDAL

"It's okay to be white," reads the sign posted in November by the Social Work building on the University of Utah campus where I teach. White poster, fine black letters in Arial font. The sign disappears in a day, though photos are taken, passed via social media. Two posters with the slogan "Stop the Rapes, Stop the Crime, Stop the Murder, Stop the Blacks" are then taped up, each with a web address for the manifesto "Blood and Soil" written by Vanguard America. These, too, are torn down. Someone spray-paints racist epithets on a campus construction site. This is not the first time signs like this have appeared at my university, but it is the first time so many have come in such quick, relentless succession. People chart the rise of these signs against the presidential inauguration. The signs, we tell ourselves, represent a dividing line—the campus we had before the current president, the campus we have now. This, however, is only our imagination of them. In reality, it is hard to point to any one dividing line.

✻

The anxiety is that the language has been generated by one of our students, though of course such language has been appearing across campuses around the nation, which makes us both less and more relieved. We are not the writers but the written upon. Disembodied, **15** or so multiple-bodied, this language becomes emptied of meaning. The language cannot embody, we say, because this speech—so formulaic, so anonymous—is ultimately addressed into the void.

✻

But, of course, the language does embody. The language was always there, not spray-painted or posted but uncovered. The language embodies because language is always speech addressed into the void into which someone, willingly or unwillingly, steps. The language opens up another dimension of the campus: a door which was once closed, and now remains open. Less than a month after Klansmen march in Charlottesville, killing a young white female protestor with a car, weeks after the president, to nearly everyone's disbelief, says about this event, "There are very fine people on both sides," Ben Shapiro, a conservative and racial provocateur, comes to speak at my campus.

✻

The language embodies because I am repelled by and called to this sign. I am half-white: I know what the sign means, though I am also mystified by it. What, in this context, does the author mean by "be white"? A small, real warmth in the belly: some spark of recognition at the sign's dismissal of racial guilt, this spark quickly extinguished by disgust for the self-pity the sign suggests by its inability to think about anything but the priority of its condition. Sensing that "doubling of time" that the poet Lisa Robertson argues is the condition of reading, I, too, am doubled in time and meaning before the sign. I am and am not the audience for it. Unable to look away, unable to dismiss it, and on both sides, outrage.

✻

16 I am thinking about this sign because I am thinking about Paul Klee, trying to parse the monumentality of his painting *Cathedral* for a lecture on Klee I'm supposed to give at the Folger Shakespeare Library. *Cathedral*'s monumentality is actually a trick of the eye: the painting itself is only 11 ¾ × 13 ⅞ inches, the length of a poster. Many of Klee's works are modest in size, the canvases bits of cardboard pasted to wood, sometimes scraps of canvas and other leftover materials. This thrift, I learn during my research on Klee, was perhaps the result of Klee's time as a soldier in the German army, when such materials were rationed. When Klee discovered a German plane crashed in a field, cleared of its bodies, he rushed to cut off pieces of the precious linen with which the plane had been covered. He saved everything, his son, Felix, said, and even painted on the backs of other paintings. Klee, according to all who knew him, refused to waste anything.

✿

Cathedral's immensity is thus due to its visual complexity. The canvas is a series of crude white lines assembled into doors and lintels, arches, windows, rooflines, walkways, buildings upon buildings. The cathedral itself is an architectural outline ghosting a soft spatter of pastels: pink and green and yellow and pale red. *Cathedral* marries Klee's background in graphic design with painting, practices which Klee did not see or treat as distinct, much as he did not see any distinction between visual and textual art. Both, he said, were problems of time and space: problems inherent to our general practices of reading.

✿

To see *Cathedral* then is to read *Cathedral*; to see the painting, I have to learn how to read Klee. In the Metropolitan Museum of Art, I study his painting *Oriental Garden* for an hour, trying to parse his lines, until I realize that none of these lines suggest or even work in the same spatial dimension. Is the path between the garden plots he's drawn in front of or below the little buildings? Am I looking down at the garden he's envisioned or straight at it? His doors—crude black squares scribbled onto canvas—look like entrances at first, but begin to suggest broken lintels, headstones. I feel nauseous looking at the painting. The lines radiate out, intersecting only where I must imagine the two-dimensional and three-dimensional meeting. Looking at Klee's lines, I don't know where I am meant to stand; I cannot tell which dimension he wants me in. I read but can't quite follow. He writes and I struggle to read him. I almost read him. Which is to say perhaps I do not read him at all.

✡

The pleasure in Klee's paintings is that I can stand anywhere. Which is also what makes Klee, at times, terrifying to me.

✡

The 18th-century art critic Gotthold Lessing, whom Klee studied, argued that space and time are progressive: action unfolds, allows for causality, even contradiction. Painting, unlike poetry, must compress time. Its uniformity means details and action are suppressed and elided so that we can take in multiple images within the same moment. What Klee achieves as a painter is something like poetry's unfolding of time: the door opening and closing at once. The garden both above and belowground. I see all actions stilled at the same moment, and yet by being aware of the different ways of entering and following his lines, I also create progressive action. Unlike Lessing, Klee insisted that space was the truly temporal concept: it is not the depiction of time's accrual and diminishment, the body in motion that mattered, but the "process of beholding" that takes place over days. Time is not depicted so much as enacted by the viewer. To see Klee, I must read his painting as a lyric unfolding.

✡

 There is, too, a sense of progressive time at play in the racist sign. Reading it, I cross over from one consciousness to the next, from the woman who is "not" raced to the one who "is." The sign is permanent disorientation, though not pleasurable in the ways that Klee's disorientations are. I suspect few people would find racist language pleasurable based on how it reorients them in relationship to the speaker: either I am in this body with this speaker or I am in another body against the speaker. In either case, such language is meant to make one's relationship to the world clearer. This, I realize, has never been the case for me.

✲

I doubt Klee painted *Cathedral* with this in mind, but the cathedral is, historically, the site of where we evolved as readers. For centuries, monks read texts aloud: reading was *meditatio*, what clerics called "masticating" the word of God. Texts were meant to be heard, chewed, swallowed, words could thus crowd together on the vellum: reading aloud gave words their beginnings and endings, shaped sentences out of crimped masses of lines and dots. Images bloomed inside the hollows and curves of the letters themselves. Language was porous, disruptive: the rabbit cradled in the hollow of a U, the knight riding his snail down the tail of an R. Silent reading appears in the 12th century, resulting in what the medievalist Michael Camille notes was the start of a permanent split between word and image. Once we read silently, words separated, margins appeared, and the visual—once the picture inside the letters—fell along the margins.

✲

It is the margin, Camille argues, where the obscene, the fanciful, the grotesque exists: the red-bottomed "babewyn," as Chaucer called it, aping the gestures of a wise man reciting the gospel, a demon shooting an arrow into a hunched man's anus. Such images were the extra-textual.

And yet to read the word *was* to read the image: the two forms of seeing **19** combined and split as the reader hovered between the sacred and profane. No longer did the act of reading necessitate speech; instead, it deepened the pleasures of sight: words become channels for color, shape, and light.

✾

Klee's paintings do exactly this. His famous 1918 painting *Once Emerged from the Gray of the Night* is also a poem—one possibly written by Klee himself—in which squares of bright gold, purples, reds, browns, and pale green radiate inside the text's block letters. In Klee's paintings, poetry and painting become the same thing, just as seeing and reading become attached to a slim margin of difference: they collapse sign and image, destabilize notions of language authorized initially by the church. What the critic Clement Greenberg once called a kind of parody, "a burlesque" of image and text.

✾

A burlesque because, written over and over, the proliferation of any word dilutes its meaning. Because the images, once profane doodles, become a way of sanctifying what is not profane. In a sense, it is the margin that centralizes the text, that gives it its final sanctity.

✾

My university's response to the proliferation of hate speech is to say, essentially, that it is marginal: damaging in the moment, but erasable. What is not marginal, apparently, is my university's commitment to "free speech," which, the university's administrators assert in their official communications, is central to the humanist values the university stands for. These values are always and truly "free." It is a very hopeful assumption about the nature of speech and reading. It is a very loose

20 interpretation of the idea of "free." In fact, there is nothing free about the way racist language makes captives of its readers, who stumble on such speech not by design but by walking across campus. And by stumbling into such language, we become both marginalized and contained within it.

✻

IRON CHINK read the sign at Seattle's Museum of History and Industry. The sign was for an exhibition on the salmon canning machine that cleaned and butchered salmon: a machine that once put my Chinese grandfather, one of many thousands of Chinese men employed by the Alaska canning industry, out of work. My mother is on the board of MOHAI: some years ago, she was distressed by the title of the exhibition. "Can you believe they can't see what's wrong with it?" my mother shouted at me over the phone. I could. I could entirely see why white board members wouldn't see the problem with the posters. My mother paused. "Just think," she said, breathing into the phone. "What those kids are going to see when they go into that exhibition." And, in silence, we imagined it: the long marble stairs, the banner in red oriental typography draped across the entrance so that child after child must walk under its heading.

✻

If reading, as Klee argued, is the deepening of our awareness of time and space, it is also the deepening of our kinship with those outside ourselves, in places we do not ourselves inhabit. It is to be called into a public body of shared knowledge that we privilege when we believe we "identify" with it. When we say the experience is "relatable." And yet I relate to no one and everyone. I am called in by reading. I am shut out. It's okay to be—.

✻

The posters, and the racist graffiti, are signs of bodies in motion. This body moved through here in order to leave this for me to read. The writer is not fixed in time, only the language is. And yet coming to the sign anew, it is as if, each time, it is being spoken aloud to me. The sign has been waiting for me. It has been waiting for me forever.

*

One day in December, over lunch, my mother tells me she is sorry she moved our family from the Asian-dominated Beacon Hill in Seattle where my grandparents and great aunts and cousins live to the whiter enclave of Ravenna Avenue. "We did it for the schools," she says, "but now you are more comfortable among white people than us." The "us" in this sentence is the slap. I am not like her, her parents, my cousins. There is a little too much emphasis my mother puts on "us." The final, forceful way she places her teacup down by her bowl. I am to feel ashamed of feeling comfortable about what I have been assigned to: a space different from my mother's.

*

This space different from my mother's is evident in the refusal of the school administrator to accept her Ph.D., the cashier speaking pidgin because he believes she can't speak English, the colleagues who burden her with more and more work, something "Asian gals are good at." I have not experienced these things because I read as white: I believe this both relieves and frustrates my mother. It is the line of racism that divides her from me, makes the passage of my body through the world easier than hers. It also makes her rage at me more vicious, poignant, solitary. Kicking in our front glass door one night, screaming because I didn't leave the porch light on for her. It terrified me. So much so, that at age sixteen, I would hide in a closet to avoid her when she was angry.

*

And yet. Though I believe I read as white, I go into the athletic store today and one of the staff asks about my country of origin. "Here," I tell her. "Here where?" she responds, looking at me as if I've just mentioned some unseen point on a map. As soon as I feel I am to be

22   read one way I am reminded of being read another. I am a constant unfolding of possibilities, lines radiating from lines.

✲

There was no *less* to my mother's rage, no sense of stop. And no apology for it after: the anger was to be forgotten, just as it was to remain hers, the result of a world only she understood and carried with her on her skin and clothing, a scent only she could wear: not her white husband, not her white daughter.

✲

"It's okay to be white," the sign says, and some cold, shameful part of me comes into being, is quickly suppressed. Both halves are called to, though of course I am already a whole. I am wholly her daughter. Racist speech demands that the reading subject not imagine herself to be indeterminate. And yet racist speech works because it triggers in the reader the anxiety that something in her *is* indeterminate. Reading these signs across campus, I am being called into a body always asked about its allegiances. I must ask my whole body to reject this speech.

✲

In many ways, reading these racist signs, no part of me at all suffers except my awareness of my proximity to those who will. A memory: riding in a cab across town to pick my parents up at their hotel. Alone with me, the cabbie is voluble, flirtatious. When we reach the hotel, however, he falls silent as my parents slide into the back and I move to the passenger seat. That's when I see it. The little web tattooed on the wing of flesh between his thumb and index finger, in which, at the center of the web, nestles a swastika.

✲

Klee's argument was that we can render the abstract only through graphic symbols. Only the figure, the sign, was able to be disseminated as knowledge. The essence of the typographical shape, he argued, was spiritual: an energy that could be translated by the reader, but only as a marker for what the artist, at the moment of creation, felt. We read the word as one. We experience the word, however, privately, conjoined and also separated by our language. We grieve together and apart.

✿

"I am not at all graspable in this world," Klee writes in 1920 in *Ararat*, a journal published on the occasion of Klee's first one-man show in Munich. It's hard not to wonder what this Swiss German artist worried about, after the Nazis closed the Bauhaus school in which he taught. Klee wasn't Jewish but he was accused of being so. His art was labeled "subversive" and in 1937 seventeen of his paintings were displayed in the famous Nazi "Degenerate Art" exhibition in Munich. Monographs of his work were burned. The Dusseldorf Academy, which hired him after the Bauhaus closed, let him go; Klee fled Germany and settled in Bern. And yet Klee seems to have been merely annoyed by all of this, what he termed "the people's stupidity." Perhaps his aloofness, his resignation to the aesthetics in fashion at the time, his years of being sheltered by art institutes, helped him remain indifferent to the rise of the National Socialists. "It seems unworthy of me to undertake anything against such crude attacks," he wrote in 1933 to his wife. "For even if it were true that I am a Jew and came from Galicia that would not affect my values as a person or my achievement by an iota." Disdainful of the Germans, Klee doubted the efficacy of the Nazis to follow through on their extremist views. Perhaps he couldn't let himself believe it.

✿

I don't think *Cathedral* is a reflection of Klee's belief in any particular faith, but rather a reflection of his fascination with the spiritual quality of

24 the line. In 1922, Klee wrote of "the original human tragedy": the vivid, mobile spirit wrestling with the impotence of the body, each tugging on the other. One weights, the other strains. And the line is the medium connecting the two. "Half captive, half winged, each part [of a person]," Klee wrote, "becomes aware of the tragedy of its incompleteness..."

✿

I am, by including this information about Klee in this particular essay, taking these quotes out of context, and in this way overwriting the space of the reader's imagination of Klee. This, too, seems similar to Klee's own project, in which the observer stands at the nexus of multiple dimensions: a window opening onto a garden which is itself a doorway into a grave.

✿

"The university does not tolerate hateful speech or discrimination against any part of our campus community," reads the University of Utah's official statement about the racist signs in a breathtaking example of synecdoche that elides all student bodies into one, compressing us within its architecture, as if the very building had a voice, unlike certain of the administrators, and very much unlike the students, who only have themselves to speak to.

✿

If there is any genius in spray-painting a racist slur on the scaffolding of a building, it is to re-author a space over which the writer is assumed to have no social hold. To write a racist slur on a building is to challenge the audience able to move through that place freely, to reclaim ownership by authoring it as implicitly white. The fact this language exists on a campus, on a religious building, on a community center is of course to deride the values, as well as the bodies, they contain. The writing turns the buildings into a caricatured vision of themselves. But perhaps another unintentional genius exists, one in which the racist language reminds us that the environment itself is a product of racism: this speech is not **25** marginal, but central. The racist writing proves this language has served the white audience in a system—an architecture—so pervasive as to be invisible. The language becomes a call to arms: Do you accept this speech? Do you accept this building, this university, this pedagogy as manifestations of that speech? If so, you cannot dismiss the language by erasing the word, you must dismantle the building.

✻

The appearing and disappearing racist signs remind me of a conversation I had years ago with a friend, an art historian who writes about public spectacles of torture. My friend was telling me about our students' use of Yik Yak: a social media app that allows people to post temporary, anonymous comments online which are then tagged to their location. To use Yik Yak, you map out a location on the app and then watch the comment bubbles attached to the grid rise and burst in gleaming succession. The app's founders began Yik Yak with college students in mind, to give shy classmates a platform on which to express themselves. How many hilarious and brilliant things, the site's founders said, are lost because the person is too frightened to say them aloud? My friend and I zoom in on the University of Utah to find out. "This party sucks and I want a burrito," one student moans. "Mormons can eat my ass," declares another.

✻

You can't use Yik Yak anymore because the app is dead. Anyone reading this can guess why. At the University of Missouri, a student used the app to threaten to shoot black students. At Western Washington, a white male student wrote "Let's lynch her" about a black student leader. Once a company worth around $400 million, Yik Yak, launched in 2013, shut down in May 2017. It lasted less than four years.

✻

26 Yik Yak, for the time it existed, operated as a margin: an opening onto a campus through which the disembodied emotions of its students could become embodied: loneliness, hunger, desire, jealousy, frustration, joy graphically, if momentarily, attached to the buildings that both cloak and house them. These voices altogether became an architecture. Yik Yak was a reminder we always write the spaces that impose their meanings upon us.

✽

What is more meaningful: the inside or the outside of the cathedral? Inside is for worshippers; outside for warding off those who would hurt the true believers inside. For this reason, the Gothic cathedral's outside was decorated with monsters: gargoyles and monkeys, demons. Like the filigreed animals proliferating inside of manuscripts, they were the twisted margin that marked the spiritually liminal space through which the believer must enter. Doors and windows, lintels, the openings of letters, but also the eye, the mouth, the nostrils, the anus: all were places where the lewd, the criminal, the demonic might penetrate. They opened out, but they also opened in.

✽

The university, too, opens out and in. The university, like the internet, is a space of potential transformation, endless openings and gateways. And yet the buildings on which the racist words appear have been built with money donated by the Charles Koch Foundation, which has pledged $10 million for the future Marriner S. Eccles Institute for Economics and Quantitative Analysis. This institute will look out onto a courtyard on which, in spring, students will sit in semicircles to discuss *The Republic* and *Paradise Lost* on stone benches paid for by the mining industry. All of which is to say that the center of the university is in constant contention with its political margin; that over years, center and margin have, for many critics, become the same thing; **27** that I insist on believing in the mission of the university, even if the tension between what it purports to value and what it is pressured to value means I do not really love universities themselves.

✿

When I think about why I am drawn to *Cathedral*, it is partly because of what it anticipates. Perhaps there is no way we can look at German painting between the 1920's and 30's and not see the future question of the Holocaust writhing inside, which is Jorie Graham's argument in her poem "Buchenwald," about Klimt's 1911 painting, which of course does not reference the future German concentration camp of the same name. Looking at these paintings, we try to read the future hidden within and alongside them, a future not even the artists themselves could guess at. We cannot separate the art from the history it both contains and creates, which is a way of saying that we also distrust the art we love when it can neither redress the horrors of war, nor anticipate them.

✿

The racist signs on my campus remind me that I do not read my country well, that my being sheltered by the university has narrowed and protected me to the point that I do not even read my institution well; that, like Klee, my practical ability to anticipate the violence of where I live and what I am has been diminished. Or perhaps, surrounded by a lifetime of such racist language, I have become numb to it. I have trained myself over years not to read the words in front of me, so that I can move through all these various rooms and halls. I exist inside my country's language. I do not read the words that encapsulate me.

✿

We call Klee's paintings poetic, meaning some element of his paintings elude us even as the symbols he uses are so familiar. Those childish

28 depictions of walls, pitched roofs for houses. Such language is meant for everyone. But other shapes recur: private, obsessive scratches and hatch marks, letters like Anglo Saxon runes. They suggest meaning but do not reveal it. The excruciating detail of a mind I love and cannot fathom. I keep on reading, scratching away for an intimacy. Art, Klee insisted, is a becoming. It is never an arrival.

✣

According to Klee: the eye must "graze away the surface... sharpening one part after the other... The eye follows the paths established for it in the work." Though *Cathedral* is a painting of a building, the lines draw spaces that are, effectively, empty: the building, shadowed with red and yellow and pink, suggests anyone can enter it, but the eye makes it hard to find the one entrance or the escape. All of it penetrable and impenetrable at once.

✣

My mother's rage has haunted and continues to haunt me. I was the child who opened into it, who was defined by it. I knew that for her being Chinese was the first point of entry to understanding her, whereas being half-Chinese was only one point of entry to understanding me. Subtle, perceptual difference that my white appearance allowed me: to some, I was the cathedral of many doors and windows, my mother the garden with its linked buildings, ancient and isolated. The door that may also be a window. The window that was equally a grave.

✣

I want to go back to my earlier argument, that the racist speech on campus is not the margin but the center. My very existence might suggest the possibility that margin and center are false juxtapositions: there is no space in which only one language exists. At best, we are all openings and goings. I don't know exactly what constitutes this whiteness that

deems itself "okay," just as I don't know exactly what would constitute   **29**
its opposite other than the experience of racism, which is not something
I want to build a life, or a personality upon. Perhaps—reading over this
last sentence—the desire not to shape my life primarily around my
experience of prejudice is the belief I can somehow avoid it, even as I
know I cannot avoid it, even as I know this belief, irrational, existing
outside of space and time, is perhaps the very definition of my whiteness.

❀

The very definition, too, possibly the source, of my mother's rage.

❀

No matter what, you will see something other than the form. I cannot
control, cannot retrain you. I mean restrain you. You will go on outside
me, without me, peering in the little window from where you have
been locked out.

❀

The slap in my relationship with my mother is understanding some
part of me will never be her daughter. If I looked more Chinese, this
might not have been a problem, but I don't. She and I ignore this point
of contention, in pursuit of some greater truth of our love for each
other. And yet to say we do not love each other because of our racial
differences is also a lie. Still, something holds us apart. I don't even think
there is a language adequate to express that loss at our center. Perhaps
this is about race, perhaps not. But race certainly makes our private
experiences more private. I love you. I believe that. It's okay to be—.

❀

There is always the desire to go further, Klee said: a sign, a symbol
that will put the object to rest behind the eye or mind. What is art but
the pursuit of that symbol? What is reading but the belief you can
understand what's been put before you?

*

Here is *Cathedral*. It is a wash of pastels, a maze of white. It is a building without doors and windows, or of only doors and windows. It has no center. It is all center. I don't know where to stand, looking at the painting. Perhaps I never will. *Cathedral* assures me of nothing. But I can stand and admire the technique, I can absorb the colors, Klee's ecstatic, expansive vision. The red, the yellows, the blues, the white. I can wander the corridors and never gain entrance. Look into it. Look harder. The trick of the painting is believing you have seen all the way through. ❧

Paisley Rekdal is the author of The Broken Country (University of Georgia Press). Her book Nightingale will be published by Copper Canyon Press in May.

PAUL KLEE

Cathedral, 1924, watercolor and oil on paper mounted on
cardboard, mounted on wood panel, 11¾ × 13⅞ inches
The Phillips Collection, Washington, DC. Acquired 1942
© 2018 Artists Rights Society (ARS), New York

ROPED TOGETHER

DAN ALTER

Secretly I stopped breathing. The whole world was alone. Have
you also heard we harbor more microbes than our own cells? Their
generations becoming, becoming in our linings. I could have left. I
roped myself to myself & stayed up making sure of the air.

Maybe time is the main problem. As far as we go.

Morning congregation: lift-gate & hand-dolly, the incoming long
cucumber, soft melons in crates. Data signed on the side of a bus;
cars ebbing at the stop; a schoolgirl leans back on high heels like ice
skates. Should I shave my head yet? Frida Kahlo as Tequila, really,
her truck passes. The dark pushed me out early again; don't need
daylight to wake, just the smell of my self burning.

During the war Braque (May 13, 1882) would be shot in the head &
left for dead. In the postscript, Picasso (October 25, 1881) said "at the
time of the mobilization, I accompanied them to the railway station at
Avignon. I never found them again." Them, meaning really, Braque.

I'm wobbling between how many kinds of time? The man whose
poem I'm stealing emailed me he's not writing. Now he just paints.
His book left a glowing location in my year. Pre-holiday house in a
preparation fever; as I retreated, the almost-full moon.

They were breaking everything into shapes. Time becoming
space. They wore blue workers overalls, they stopped signing their
canvases. Studios within minutes. Nothing was the star as the bowl
of fruit or violin was dismantled, all the colors becoming brown.

After their six or so years, that was it. Now we would be looking

through everything, pieced together, coming apart. Anyway the
camera had taken over the surface. & would dismantle it from the
other side. Piercing with microscopy, panning out to God's eye.

Picasso: "I miss you, what's happened to our walks & our exchange
of feelings…. Write me & I'll write you often."

We could try to put the genie back in the bottle.

"In those years Picasso and I said things to each other that nobody
will ever say again, that nobody could say any more … We were like a
pair of mountain-climbers roped together."

The first time they tried to take out my wisdom teeth, no matter how
much Novocaine I could feel things cracking. Later they subtracted
me. Letters in a word going backward: incision in my time. When I
woke I walked out with holes. Does removal let in more present tense?

No soundtrack in the track-lit air. On the expensive wall, stills from
the movie of your soul. I wrote the movie of your soul & tried to
remember where I heard it from. Looked and looked at leaves, one
repeating greenness. Sometimes a song comes along like a cylinder
of time; go inside & get warm.

"Almost every evening, either I went to Braque's studio or Braque came
to mine. Each of us had to see what the other had done during the day."

Passing cars are dotted lines. The reunion is waiting the only place
it can, in the past. I've often been mistaken. Where there are no
windows, someone's pictures of Morocco; a parked Subaru just
bounced backward, no driver inside.

How much of the relationship is what the time allows? Liquid motion

of vehicles going. Fighting the urge to read your face as denouement.
While walking the birds back to water, the sky became a sketchbook.

Where Braque's studio walls converged, a future of a guitar, long
gone. Picasso set aside his harlequins & women swollen with
emotion to follow the scissors. Africa was coming in. Did they really
derive it as if numbers?

Woman With a Mandolin, 1910, Braque: the higher her body, the
more her shoulders spread into shimmers. Head & neck prism
& become brown air. Her body is breaking into music, the music
comes from a tunnel in her hands. On one set of notes I have
survived, & here is another playing a hundred years away. Or are
they the same notes in an oval, the olive color of shadows in oil.
Her head, vaguely a bull's, is bent toward her instrument. Which is
making her into strings of time.

Traffic blurs by as a pattern you step out of. Unstoppable, in one
sense; in another as fragile as tissue. I'm trying to make my own
museum. Paper collar on my hot glass keeps falling down.

If minutes are a fabric, do they shimmer when they catch light?
Little ink lassos, but it always gets away. They used to call it a soul,
then everything became a particle. Burnt my finger on the pot lid,
still stinging. Really a little rain again? The tiny wheels of human
time spinning: in that scale we are at sea.

Picasso was already the hero. Their dealer paid him sevenfold what he
paid Braque for a canvas. But the housepainter's son studied the way
light went to pieces on a rooftop. His landscape Matisse dismissed:
"little cubes." Then they began to subtract color, & their names.

"During those years the difference didn't count...when I was so close to

Picasso, there was a time when we could hardly tell our pictures apart." **35**

How far could they separate pigment from its pin? Braque began making paper sculptures, space could become flat again. We are mounted in the one dimension. Always imagining our freedom of motion.

After Braque, Picasso developed his "two tracks": one told his stories, the other continued shattering into facets. As if trying to have a conversation between himself.

We still haven't talked about the baby we won't have. Its unexistence a hollow in you. Every month another ova & uterine lining sheds into the past. My friends have receded until they are vague ideas, lakeshores & subways, varieties of sleep. Still air, high ceilings, paintings, quietly. Is it too late for me to listen to color moving in oils?

Woman With a Mandolin, 1910, Picasso: From her balcony a city listens. Her hands have disappeared into the pinwheel of curves revolving near the center, at her chest. Mouth puckered to hold back the story. More of her & only half a mandolin which floats into rooftops. I miss the hundred years her moon rises on, while they were still seeing each other every day.

In the book on my table two players turn to face each other as much as they can from the flatness. Music going into the future to find us. Each of us with our own station streaming. Now do we understand?

Picasso: "It's not a reality you can take in your hand. It's more like a perfume—in front of you, behind you, to the sides. The scent is everywhere but you don't quite know where it comes from."

Dan Alter has been published in Pank, Field, *and elsewhere. He has been a fellow of the Arad Arts Project, and his poetry appeared in Issue No. 105.*

POLYPTYCH

BEN GREENMAN

1

He went out in the morning to look at a painting. It was early, so he had set his alarm, but he didn't even need it—ten minutes before it was supposed to ring, his eyes came open, both at once. Was that usually the way? Did some people open one eye and then, after a while, the other? How many people woke but kept their eyes closed, trying to stay inside the cylinder of sleep? These were all good questions, but he needed to be out of the house to see the painting.

2

Most days he collected the newspaper and began his day by reading it in the chair beside his bed. This was a holdover from the days when he had been married, and when something about the presence of his wife in the bed—her beauty, mainly, which was far greater as she slept than when she was awake—had stung him. He had needed to be out of that bed, on his feet, brushing teeth, checking his reflection in the mirror, performing various ablutions and eliminations, and finally going for the paper, which allowed him to settle into the activities of the broader world. Only then could he return to his wife and wake her, an act that shifted her face from the supreme beauty of its sleeping state into the more complex, not entirely lovely aspect it possessed when awake. She knew he was disappointed seeing her awake. It must have been obvious **37** from his expression. In the face of that knowledge he burrowed into the newspaper even more aggressively. His wife had laughed harshly at his attempts to escape. "Are you trying to read under the words?" she had said, and then said that she was going to order a needlepoint sampler with that question on it. That was her ironic way of dismissing one of her own questions or remarks, though, in fact, it was a strategy for suggesting that the question or remark had been particularly profound. She devoutly believed that many of the things she said deserved to be framed and hung on the wall.

3

In the past the newspaper was central to his morning ritual. But there was no more wife whose sleeping face was too beautiful for him to look upon—she had left him and moved far away—and at any rate today was a special day. Today was the day he was going to see the painting. For a moment he was not sure how he would adjust his ritual without destroying it, but then inspiration struck. He knew what he would do. He would bring the newspaper in from the front lawn, but he would not read it.

4

He stood outside checking the sky. Light was beginning to come into it, and when he saw that it was clear—not quite blue yet but the color of a bruise healing—he decided to walk into town. As he went back inside, he bent to collect the paper and saw the top headline, something about the murder of a young man down at the waterfront. He wished he hadn't looked. The young man had the same name as a man he had once known, though it could not have been the same man. The man he had known was older than him, and was long dead. That man had

38   been a professor of his in college. He had introduced him to another man, a lawyer who had given him his first job, and that lawyer had in turn introduced him to the man who had gotten him interested in art. This third man was the uncle of the woman who had become his wife. He thought of this third man as his mentor. This was many years ago, in another city.

5

The other city had a world-renowned museum. He had visited it only twice, once with the man who had been introduced to him by the man—his mentor—who had been introduced to him by the professor, and once on his own. The second visit was the one that had truly hooked him. He had stood in front of a canvas that was bright orange at the top and dark brown at the bottom and all gradations going downward. He had imagined that the orange was life and that the brown was death, and that the canvas was a kind of clock that showed the passage of time. He tried to locate himself on the canvas. Back then, he had been nearer to the orange.

6

He dressed, remembering the woman who had been with him a few evenings before. She was a lawyer from the office down the hall from his own law office. "We have lots in common," she said, though this was not in fact the case. She specialized in taxes. His firm specialized in rules governing the sale and purchase of commodities. She was short and brunette. He was tall and had been blond when his hair was present, though now it was mostly gone, down to a hint at each temple. She was a woman. He was a man. Maybe that was what she meant. He had taken her to dinner twice at the same excellent seafood place (portions the proper size, price expensive but not too expensive), and the third time she had nodded as he asked but then said she was in the mood to **39** eat something else, and that she would be over at his place after work. It had taken him longer than it should have to see how forward she was being. It had taken him until he nodded, told her he would see her around seven, walked back to his desk, and started reviewing a case that revolved around the question of interstate commerce. Then it hit him and he blushed crimson.

7

She had been at his house at seven. She had been undressed by seven-ten, had him in the same vulnerable state by seven-fifteen, and had put him through his paces until nine o'clock, at which point they had ordered pizza and eaten it while they watched a true-crime television show. The episode they watched also concerned the waterfront. "I don't like it when people talk about violence," she said. He had agreed but she had stopped him. "I don't know if you know what I mean," she said. "I mean that I don't like it because I think that violence can be a great and positive thing if used correctly. A show of force, even rough, even cruel, can be compelling." She was being forward again. Suddenly it was eleven o'clock, post-paces again. They slept perpendicular to each other.

8

The morning he woke up with the woman he noticed her beauty while sleeping paled to her beauty while awake. It was her eyes that were lively and sharp. He woke her quickly. She made use of him one more time before work. That morning his ablutions and eliminations were automatic to the point of belonging not to him exactly but to the boilerplate of the universe. Now, days later, he remembered them. He even remembered his wife. That meant the presence of the woman was beginning to fade.

40

9

Valuable time was being chewed up by the jaws of idle thought. Would this sentence have made a good needlepoint sampler? He hardly had time to think about it. He hurried on the rest of his clothes and made for the door. He had to walk fast if he was going to make it. He had seen the painting before, but not in person, which meant he had not seen it at all. That was one thing that his mentor had told him many years ago. A painting was not simply an image. A painting was a thing. When it was reproduced in a newspaper or magazine, it received a push toward death—a small push, a weak push, but still a push. It was fixed by the impersonal eye of the camera, and as such was memorialized. When a painting was viewed in person, it exploded outward from its square on the wall, in color, in texture, in size, even in smell (though, the man said, the smell of a painting operated on a viewer at a not entirely conscious level). In person a painting grabbed you by the lapels. In a newspaper or a magazine, it meekly offered you its lapels to grab.

10

He had seen this painting in the newspaper the previous day—that newspaper he had collected in the early morning hours and brought back to the kitchen table where his female visitor was already sitting. She had read the front section while he had taken the rest. She had clucked her tongue at the events of the world and he had solaced himself with sports scores, the prices of stocks, the funny pages, and finally with various beautiful pictures: of dancers, of new buildings in the downtown, and finally of the painting. It was a painting of a large face, and in each eye of the face there was a large reflection of a large building, and each window of the building was itself a kind of painting. All manner of things were happening in those windows.

11 41

The article in the newspaper had not just shown the painting. It had discussed it at some length. His mentor, who had not been thrilled about the way newspapers and magazines showed paintings, had been more sanguine about the way newspapers and magazines discussed them. "The medium is language," his mentor had said, and stopped, and shook his head, as if coming free from a deep sleep. After a few long seconds, he had resumed speaking. "The medium is language even when language is not the medium." He went on to explain what he meant: that man was capable of many different acts of construction or arrangement or organization, as were other animals, but that what made them creative acts, in the commonly understood sense, is that they could be ascribed meaning through language. His mentor's disquisition lasted for nearly five solid minutes but what remained behind was mainly that initial aphorism, a perfect sampler.

12

The discussion of the painting in the newspaper had gone on at length as well, and had one point that shone brighter than the rest: in this case, it was the insight that the painting was best viewed early in the morning. It was being exhibited in the lobby of an office building a few blocks away from his own office. It had been commissioned for that space. But, as the article said, while it improved and energized that space at all times of the day, it pulsed with its truest energy in the hour after dawn. It was something about the colors and the composition, something about the size and the shape. It was something about everything about the painting. "It can be seen, and appreciated, at any hour," the article said, "but if seen during the first hours of the day, it may save your life."

13

He walked to town, wondering when next a woman would come to his house, and whether it would be the same woman from last time, and if so, if the same things would happen, and if not, what other things would happen. As he went, he tried to remember the image of the painting from the newspaper, and in particular what he thought he had seen in the windows in the building in the painting, or rather what he had imagined he had seen there, which was the same as what he believed happened in the city over the course of any several days: several births and several deaths, several acts of love and several acts of violence, a few moments of spectacularly byzantine perversion that resulted in peak experiences of passion for all involved (one character he imagined was brought to such a state of carnal excitation that she found herself temporarily unable to recall any of the seven continents, and panicked until one began to take shape in her mind, the big one in the middle, where all life had begun, she almost had the name, it was a song, Africa), a few murders, a man alone, a man back from a walk.

14

He came into town about twenty minutes past dawn and went straight to the building where the painting was being exhibited. It was being exhibited in the lobby. The lobby was locked. He knocked on the glass door. A man in a uniform was sitting in a chair reading the newspaper, his feet up on the desk beside a bank of monitors that showed empty rooms and hallways. The man in the uniform stood, walked to within three feet of the door, stopped, and pointed at a framed sign on the wall outside the glass that displayed the building's hours of business. Then he went back to his chair and his newspaper.

43

He kept knocking but now the man in the uniform did not answer. He pressed his face to the glass and squinted at the painting. He could not quite see it. He saw the outlines of the face but none of its features. The eventful windows in the building in the painting, so wonderfully rendered even in the picture in the paper, were at a difficult angle, and weakened to dull gray rectangles. He waited for a brainstorm that would help him salvage the day but no inspiration came to him. He was marooned in the sad facts of the morning, which was that he had gone out to look at a painting. It was early, so he had set his alarm, but he hadn't even needed it. And now he was not able to see that painting. He was suddenly exhausted. He was closer to the brown. He did not love the woman who had come to his home, though she had put him through his paces. He still loved the woman who had been his wife, though she had been more beautiful asleep than awake and had left him at any rate. He closed his eyes. Did some people close one eye and then, after a while, the other? How many people closed their eyes and imagined they were no longer in the world? These were all painful questions, and he stood in the space outside the glass and waited for time to pass and the building to open so he could have a lesser look at the painting he had been led to believe might save his life. ✄

Ben Greenman is the author of several books, including Don Quixotic *(Antibookclub), and the co-writer of* Questlove's Creative Quest *(Ecco).*

I SAW A PHOTOGRAPH OF A SHIPWRECK AND I KNEW

DENVER BUTSON

I saw a photograph of a shipwreck and I knew at once that it was a beehive disguised as a shipwreck that in reality all shipwrecks are beehives and vice versa I knew at once that the deck of this shipwreck was a place where we had once danced our skin tingling from beestings we didn't recognize at the time as beestings I saw a photograph of a shipwreck and I knew that it was a mansion and the waves around it were mountains and the sky around it was sky above the mansion I knew that if I took you there and pulled out the house keys the mansion would suddenly be our mansion and I would open the door the door which is suddenly our door and everyone you have ever loved would jump out from behind the furniture that they think is the furniture inside our little apartment not the furniture inside a mansion let alone our mansion and not the furniture inside a shipwreck or beehive for that matter and they would all shout we love you! at once and they would all turn to each other and talk about you and me and our lives as if we were captains of our own ship this whole time and their combined voices would be like the murmuring of thousands of bees inside a beehive disguised as a shipwreck that they think is another of our railroad apartments not a mansion on a hill underneath the sky I saw a photograph of a shipwreck and I knew all this and nothing at all and I knew that no matter how many other photographs I see it will be this one that will remain projected on the backs of my eyelids which will be disguised as drive-in movie screens when I close them every time from here on out until the last time I pull my car into the drive-in movie lot and look up at the giant screen and the shipwreck appears there like a

beehive and the speaker clipped to my driver's side window starts

buzzing like bees when you rise up out of the shipwreck just like

always.

ENNIO MORRICONE IS DISSOLVING

DENVER BUTSON

Ennio Morricone is dissolving in a field of
sunflowers. he is wearing a well-tailored suit
and heavy-rimmed glasses. his hair is slicked
back. let's call this moment *studio numero
cento*. or let's call it *study in dissolving*. let's
pretend that those mosquitoes are far-off
violins. let's pretend the breeze-rattling of
sunflower stalks is the far-off approach of
percussion. just as Ennio Morricone would
have wanted it. you might think this is
1974 or 1967. if it weren't for the fact that
Ennio Morricone looks much older now in
whatever year this is than he did back then.
from the photographs of him you have seen
back then. and yet he looks as if he might
have been standing here for centuries. the
sunflowers grow up. they turn their heads
toward the sun. *girasole* you remember from
your Italian book. *gira-ing toward the sole*.
they droop their heads and then they fall.
and Ennio Morricone is dissolving. as if he
were any of a number of *spaventapasseri*. any
of a number of scarecrows. dissolving. as
new crops of girasole grow up again from
the seeds their ancestors have dropped. and
the sun sets and rises. sets and rises.

Ennio Morricone is dissolving. and somehow holding himself as still as a daguerreotype. as if any sudden movement might cause him to shatter like glass. to burst open. and spill all his dreams. like seeds. the glass seeds. of ennio morricone's dreams. scattering everywhere. onto the ground and into the wind. as if they weren't even his dreams to have. as if he weren't even here to dream them.

SMOKE

DENVER BUTSON

the accordionist wishes he were an acrobat
the acrobat wants to be a tightrope walker
the tightrope walker longs to be a ballerina
the ballerina wishes she were an opera singer
the opera singer would love to be a painter
the painter says he would rather be a poet
the poet dreams of being a mariachi trumpeter
the mariachi trumpeter longs to be a filmmaker
the filmmaker would like a chance to be a fire-eater
the fire-eater imagines himself a photographer
the photographer longs to be a juggler
the juggler is hoping to become a scarecrow
the scarecrow would rather be a puff of pollen dust

and the puff of pollen dust
doesn't know that it is not smoke

Denver Butson's fourth book is the sum of uncountable things (Deadly Chaps Press). He lives in Brooklyn, N.Y.

DIRECTOR'S CUT

TONI MARTIN

When the scene opens, I am standing on the platform of the BART station, which is outdoors, in the middle of a loud freeway, facing the track for the San Francisco train. The platform is two stories above ground level here. The city is just visible to the left, pearlized skyscrapers on a floating Oz. Cars shoot past in front and behind me, toward my destination, or up into the East Bay Hills on the right, where fog hovers against the brooding green. Straight ahead, past the lanes of autos, the tops of the trees offer the illusion that the concrete structure, large enough for both the freeway and the train, is suspended.

This is the first time I have worked with this Japanese director. I will tell you all that I have learned. The traffic is a backdrop to my stillness. In an art film, where time flows broadly, serenely, I would not struggle, even on a packed Tokyo subway train. The director is not in a hurry for me to arrive in the city and advance the plot. He allows me time to wait, to tuck my transit card into the outside pocket of my purse, and to scan up and down the track.

Because we all have stories, I could be a woman of any age, even elderly, taking tiny steps, although as it happens, I am closing in on thirty. I look perfectly comfortable alone, not as though I were missing a partner. I do not clutch my purse or move closer to other women. And

50 you, the audience, do not have to eye the characters on the platform suspiciously, even the scraggly man wearing a plastic bag against the sudden rain. The rain itself would carry less meaning. It would not announce that this was going to be a sad movie. It would be a fact of life, that day. And tomorrow is another day.

You know that I am the main character because the camera quietly returns to me, not because I am wearing different clothes or look more glamorous than other people in the scene. Even if I had perfect skin and long shiny hair, I might be wearing a cap, or a uniform. The camera would not linger lasciviously on my face. My gaze would not announce how vulnerable I feel, if I did. I do not look directly at the camera. There may be a hint, in the way I shift my purse, that if given a choice, I might be elsewhere, but I am not straining under my burden. There is no impatient sigh.

There might be a few moments before the soundtrack starts, and when it does, it might be only the swoosh of the cars on the wet pavement and the giggles of schoolgirls, if there were schoolgirls. I have ear buds, but not in my ears, unless there is music. If there is music, it might be '50s jazz or Western classical music, like in a Murakami novel. Or it could be electronic. It would not be a "hit song" or "our song." It would not bother you, if you did not recognize it. You do not expect to know this person, the "I" on the platform, right away or to be attracted by my choices. You expect me to be honest. I have no expectations of you, because I am a character in a movie.

Finally, the train comes. Enough time has passed that you and I are both relieved, although you are still anxious for me. You want me to have an adventure and ideally find love. You scan the people in my train car, looking for likely candidates. They are speaking in many languages, including Japanese, which I don't understand.

I sit down by a window and you expect to see countryside. Even if the film were set in Tokyo, at some point, on some train, I would look **51** out at terraced rice paddies and small farms, beyond the motley roofs. The landscape and the train itself are a cultural space in the heart, a home that you, the audience, carry with you.

The aerial shot of New York City in American films is intended to link us in the same way, but it doesn't: not if, like me, you don't know New York City. Maybe the skyscrapers in New York and the rice fields in Japan are both aimed at a global audience. Perhaps, unlike me, the Japanese audience grows restless when the camera lingers on the rural landscape. At any rate, the train soon dips into a tunnel and there is nothing to see.

Now I arrive in the city, San Francisco, and ride the escalator up to the street. In this Japanese movie, there is no handsome Uber driver for me to meet cute as I exit, but no street person camped at my feet, either. You are surprised to see that it has stopped raining now, or perhaps it didn't rain on this side of the bay. Black clouds studded with shards of sunlight pass overhead, dressed for downtown.

Respectable small shopkeepers along Market Street are shuttering their storefronts; only sleazy joints turn on the neon and brace for drunken salarymen. I walk briskly, with purpose. The camera notices the setting sun glinting off the dome of City Hall and the pigeons under the pollarded trees. I do not encounter anyone I know along the way, to set up the next scene. I have to walk alone into the marble lobby of the concert hall, where my childhood violin teacher waits.

The first shot is of her sitting alone, reading the program. She is a completely contained woman, all in black, with a short gray bob. When I enter the frame, I look ungainly, too tall, with a ridiculous flower print shirt revealed once I remove my navy jacket. You know immediately that I could never play the violin well. But my teacher stands and embraces me. In this Japanese movie, you expect us to honor the years we spent together.

Once a year, she sends me a printed announcement of the student recital, which I do not attend. But I write her a note back, suggesting we meet for a concert. She took me with other students to my first concert, when I was a little girl. We sat in the balcony, and when I saw the musicians, I wanted to fly down and hide among them, to belong to the music. In a flashback, my classmates and I, with dark hair and navy uniforms, could turn into crows with blue-black wings—a touch of magical realism, an homage to a certain French or Italian director. Or not.

My teacher speaks English to me. You expect her to ask about my mother's health but my teacher knows she died a few years ago. It was no secret the lessons were my mother's idea and I always wanted to quit. My teacher understood us both, even then. She respected my mother's dream of a child with musical talent and she accepted that I was not that person. During the lessons, after I displayed my token effort, she played for me, or we listened to recordings together. She praised me for my sophisticated ear, so I did not turn against music. When she and my mother conferred, she did not pretend I was making rapid progress but she did not join my mother in scolding me for not practicing, either.

I ask after her son, Hiroshi, who was a few years older than me and is now a concert pianist. After my question, another flashback: a young girl stands playing a violin, next to a calm teacher. It is late afternoon and the piano behind them is in shadow, because the only light is on the music stand. (Watching later, I wince at the harsh notes the girl plays, but my arms don't feel the weight of the instrument.) When a door slams, the girl pulls the violin from her chin. A teenager in a school uniform appears and bows to his mother and the student. His silent confidence floods the scene and commands your attention. The mother, smiling, inclines her head and the girl, flustered, bows slightly.

She waits until he withdraws to raise the violin again.

My teacher responds that Hiroshi is touring in Europe at the moment. She adds that there is another grandchild in New York. The camera has returned to us in the present and you may be surprised that her face is not as bright as her voice. She misses him.

It is comfortable here, in this movie. You, the audience, accept me as a fellow traveler, not a movie star. My teacher takes my arm as we walk toward our seats. We are hearing Mahler tonight and sitting downstairs, a treat for both of us. Neither of us is so well off that we can take events like this for granted. The director will include more of the concert than you may want to hear before the plot moves on. He took violin lessons as a child, not me.

You feel the companionship of the two women, our humility, in the presence of the orchestra. At intermission, we walk out to the bar and order glasses of champagne, our traditional splurge. My teacher proposes we toast the musicians and I add our good fortune to hear them. We edge through the crowd to the glass walls, where we can look down on the street and watch the umbrellas open as the rain starts here. The light inside is golden compared to the gray street. We sip and smile. The camera stays with our reflections on the glass until the alcohol roses our cheeks. This is the director's favorite shot.

The gentle buzz from the champagne wears off before the second half of the concert ends and I fidget, rubbing my hands. It is a relief when the applause starts because you and I have lost track of the movements: whether that was a fast adagio or a slow andante. It takes my teacher and me a while to shuffle through the crowd to the exit. The fresh air is cool and damp on our faces, but it is not raining hard enough for an umbrella now. It is a weeknight and I have started to think about work tomorrow when my teacher, pushed toward the curb, slips and falls on the slick street.

53

54 She says she is fine and pulls up on the arm that I extend but she is not fine. She can't put weight on her right leg. Finally, a crisis. You welcome the sound of the ambulance approaching and the liquid red lights reflected on the wet pavement. For a moment, you wish you had chosen a Hollywood movie, one with reliable action.

After the ambulance ride and the X-ray, the doctor, another woman, confides gently that my teacher has broken her hip.

The doctor looks at the registration form and asks my teacher if they should call her son, who is listed as the emergency contact. At first she demurs, she doesn't want to bother him. But the doctor explains that after the surgery patients are not able to go home alone because walking is still difficult. One choice is inpatient rehab—a rehabilitation facility— for intensive physical therapy. In other words, there are decisions to be made. My teacher looks exhausted and bewildered. I offer to call.

The sign says "No cell phones," so I walk outside for a moment, take a break from the overheated chaos. Orange points from lit cigarettes glow and move with the smokers in the parking lot like performance art. Truthfully, the director asked me to smoke, too, but I drew the line there. Instead, I shelter beneath the building overhang because it's still drizzling and take deep breaths before I attempt to place the call. It is a crazy time difference in Switzerland, and Hiroshi is confused about who I am until I haltingly admit that I was the Wednesday student who played so badly. You feel sorry for me.

Surgery is scheduled for the morning. I explain the plan as I understand it. No, not a nursing home, the doctor assured us and I assure Hiroshi, although I am not at all sure about the difference between a "rehabilitation facility" and a nursing home and he can tell. He asks anxious questions until I admit that I trust the doctor because she has tickets for the Mahler tomorrow night and then he sighs.

My teacher and I spend most of the night in the emergency room,

she snoring sweetly on the gurney, except when she moves and moans; **55**
me seated next to her, trying to stay awake enough to guard our purses
and watch for developments. This is an opportunity for a parade of
bit characters and salty nurses. There is a Yakuza guy with tattooed
arms bulging in a sleeveless undershirt in every movie this director
makes. I thought he would show in this scene but I don't see him. I see
a translucent young man, bald from chemotherapy. And a stout black
cop, his uniform shirt pulled out over his belt and holster. I stay with
my teacher as she is transferred to a room and wait until daylight when
they roll her off to surgery. I am dismayed at how old she looks under
the fierce lights. Then I trudge back to BART.

The director does not follow me to my small apartment just yet.
This is a good choice, because I need to sleep. I was happy that the
script didn't call for me to feed a cat here, either—I am not that woman.
Eventually, you will see my apartment through Hiroshi's eyes, his
judgment about the bars on the kitchen window and the absence of
any musical instrument.

When he arrives, thirty-six hours later, I am at his mother's bedside.
Her leg is in a contraption and elevated after the operation. In this
Japanese movie, the hospital rooms are not pink and cushioned but
sparsely furnished with narrow beds and straight-backed chairs. His
mother is dozing and we are both reluctant to wake her, so we don't
speak. Now he is distinguished and married, less available to me than
ever, but in the hospital no one knows him or me and they assume we
are a couple. He is the son and I am with him.

While his mother sleeps, we head to the cafeteria for a coffee, and
you suspect by the way his eyes follow me that we will arrange to meet
again. You are correct. In the cafeteria, the light bounces off the shiny
linoleum and Formica and his glossy hair. Again, people are speaking
in many languages—the director remembers a polyglot San Francisco.

56 A child cries above the general din and Hiroshi and I lean closer.

I study his tired face, the texture of his woolen jacket. He is the most famous person I know, yet we are strangers. Our hesitant conversation skirts murky banks of loneliness and dislocation. At one point, you close your eyes to rest into his quiet voice. When you open them, the little girl who has stopped crying wanders into the frame, her face swollen, hair askew. We watch her with you.

I have his mother's purse, with the keys to her house, and he does not know the way from the hospital. So we both go. He opens the door while I wait on the porch, the way I used to wait for the student before me to finish. Inside, nothing has changed. The violin case is in the entry, along with a briefcase of music books, ready for my teacher to grab on her way out. Around the hulking grand piano in the living room, music stands cluster like skeletons-in-waiting. I sit on a chair, my place, not the sofa, my mother's place. The director makes you wait with me, uncertain whether Hiroshi will ask me to stay. We can hear him running water, opening doors. Finally, he calls to me and I stand up, steadying myself on the side of the piano.

Let me warn you: eventually, I confess my childhood crush. In my contract, I agreed to take my clothes off, yet in this type of movie you can't count on naked sex, even with this age-appropriate potential partner. He and I wrestle with our mixed feelings and you will not be sure whether we will fall in love or never see each other again or both.

Each outcome, the blossom and the withered bud, is equally plausible. Our feelings are complicated and there is no obvious default convention. There are also no best friends to explain our emotions to us. Like you, I can only read Hiroshi's face and listen to his words. The concentration is like synchronized swimming high in the air, a slow aerial dance without a net.

If all else fails, the camera will seek order and beauty to comfort you: Hiroshi, in white cotton undershorts and T-shirt playing Chopin, **57** white eggs lined up on the kitchen counter, shadows of trees outside.

I put myself at his disposal for the two days he stays. I mostly telework anyway, and this is one of those movies, an interval out of time. He must have connections here, friends he grew up with, musicians, but he doesn't contact them.

I drive him out to the rehabilitation facility and tour with him, asking the questions a woman would ask, about laundry and food. He asks about the physical therapy. We walk in the garden, roses just leafing out, memorial plaques on every tree and bench.

"Only for a week or so," he repeats.

I nod.

The next day, they are late transporting his mother and we have to leave for the airport before she arrives. She will be disappointed not to see him again. At the terminal, when I drop him off, I promise to go right back to check on her. He hesitates with the door open but the cop is already motioning me to move on.

It feels different to drive back to the facility alone. I did not understand at first why the director made me sit in the car, hands on the wheel, once I had parked. But you can see that it is a good moment, he was right. I stare straight into the camera, stunned and exhausted.

When I find my teacher's room, she is crying softly. I don't ask her why but she says that the ride was uncomfortable and there was a delay in getting her pain medication started. She has just received it. I sit down next to the bed and take her hand, which is cold. I fuss in her belongings bag and find a robe, which I lay over her shoulders. She thanks me for coming, for all my help. I thank her for her patience with me as a child and she laughs. The medicine is in her system.

We are on break from filming now. I expect my teacher to recover, and the final scene could show us back at the concert hall another year, but she could also have an unexpected complication and the scene could take place in a cemetery, where Hiroshi and I stand at his mother's graveside under a cherry tree in bloom. Maybe the Yakuza guy is a fellow mourner. He took violin lessons once. A Japanese movie of this type is unpredictable, except that cherry blossoms symbolize the fragility and beauty of life.

I am using the time to watch other Japanese films. As the credits roll, I puzzle over what I have seen, whether their stories were enough of a movie, and I imagine how you will feel watching ours. I hope you will think our movie is just right. It would help if they translated the lyrics of the poignant song that plays over the titles.

In your online review, you may complain the pace was too slow, that the story meandered and you did not know what to expect. You may accuse the director of flirting with obscurity. But I predict at least three stars, because there will be moments that resonate. You have also drunk champagne without knowing what the night would bring.

And you, also, appreciate the illumination of a small, unsettled life. ❦

Toni Martin has been published in The Threepenny Review, Bellevue Literary Review, *and* Berkeley Monthly, *among other places. Her nonfiction work "Still Water" was published in Issue No. 64.*

PLEASURE OR BUSINESS?

MIRA ROSENTHAL

And I answer, "No. I'm in Poland for the poetry."
But over beers in a basement filled with blue
shadows caught on the crumbling brick baleen
of the wall, strangers keep claiming, "I'm related to you."
For somewhere distant within the sea of the gene
pool they want a Jewish sister, want a brew

that is anything but filtered, something saline
and medicinal in the act of saying it's true,

something passive in the fact of the glass
in my hand, while down the road tourists perform
their rites to the history, singing within the frame
of a museum's reconstructed shelter on the vast
Birkenau prairie. In this belly, in this swarm
of talk, I drink the gravel ballast of my name.

Mira Rosenthal's most recent book is The Local World *(Kent State University Press). She is an assistant professor of creative writing at Cal Poly.*

A SERIES OF DIRECTIONS NONE ABANDONED (FRAME I)

RUSTY MORRISON

toward Agnes Martin's "far away love"

"was" is a soft word when mouthed gone unreachable in wide swathes
of a muted blue-violet with horizontal bars unevenly placed here
escape can be an "is" achievable in paint "was" is the damage I do to
this artwork on the gallery wall "created serene paintings composed
of grids and stripes" is the curator's modest curatorial frame for a
framed canvas that accepts what is given when a painting purely
absorbs I call it painstaking and painless as nothing escapes a surface
I paint over the painting with soft-focus I fail it as Agnes Martin
might have expected and condoned I am the flaw holding tight to
these long horizontal gaps in front of me as if I can avoid falling into
the blue-violet field which has no interest in moving anywhere but
away from all who view it drawing us with it as we choose or fail
to choose still we're absorbed we move beyond ourselves I'd like to
believe this as if "moving" were an acceptable notion not a flawed
hackneyed gerund of kitsch that the painting accepts as it accepts
all failings that it sucks into its maw churning as does a carnivorous
pitcher-plant when an insect has stepped on its cupped leaf and
fallen into a sticky drowning ingestion into plant energy that the
insect becomes just as this painting now consumes me

Rusty Morrison is the co-publisher of Omnidawn. Her most recent book is Beyond the Chainlink
(Asahta Press).

DON'T GO TO STRANGERS

MATTHEW JEFFREY VEGARI

n the living room, two couples sit on opposite leather couches, one
hand-in-hand, fingers laced around fingers, the other slightly apart,
shoe heels touching on the shag carpet below. Another dinner party
of friends and coworkers has ended, and the couples carry on even as
they begin to forget their words. The women finish off tall glasses of
champagne, while the men gulp down warm bottles of beer. It is after
ten, and everyone has gone home for the evening, with the exception
of Alice and Trevor Jackson, who are not overstaying their welcome.
On the contrary, the hosts, Allen and Jane Mitchell, are pleased to
have friends linger behind. Between the marriages of the Jacksons and
Mitchells there are three girls and a boy, two children per couple, who
are upstairs sleeping in the case of the Mitchells, or, for the Jacksons,
a few miles east, watching a movie with a babysitter who has been told
that things could end at any hour.

Allen Mitchell takes a final sip of his beer and squeezes his wife's
hand. It has been a long day for them both, and now they can relax and
enjoy a drink or two with their friends, maybe a slice of cake. They
worked hard to entertain twenty people in their home, and things went
well, very well in fact. The guests arrived on time; dinner was served
without complaint; the thunderstorm, once predicted to ruin the evening,
postponed itself for another day. Allen looks across the room to Trevor

62 who is telling a story about two of his students, one he has told before about a spontaneous wrestling match. Allen appreciates that his friend of many years can enjoy this night with him. He has known Trevor through their graduations—high school and college—and their weddings, and tonight the celebration of his own promotion registers another victory. In a way, he thinks, they are like brothers. He has seen Trevor grow from a young boy with a thin frame to a towering man, a father, with large arms and a sizeable stomach. And, much like brothers, their relationship has changed over time. Last week, after discussing Trevor's upcoming thirty-sixth birthday over lunch, he became conscious of a pause in their conversation—a lull—as the two of them looked out the window and chewed their roast-beef sandwiches. He found comfort in the familiarity of their friendship, because it eliminated the need to say anything at all; the silence itself was full.

Jane laughs at Trevor's story, one that gets funnier each time he tells it. She looks from Trevor to Alice, who grins uncomfortably, perhaps worried that her husband's old joke will fall flat. Jane is not fond of Alice Jackson, but appreciates how her own husband gets along with Trevor. Trevor is taller than Allen, better at sports, the one prone to over-drinking at gatherings like this. Allen is smarter and handsomer, his hair showing no signs of thinning. Trevor is a gym teacher, and Allen is, now, a vice president. Unlike the two men, however, Jane and Alice do not complement each other. Their friendship was not formed organically, and instead they met out of an expectation for spouses. As she knows many people do, Jane maintains her friendship with Alice out of convenience: for the sake of their husbands, it is simply easier for them to be friends than adversaries. For a moment, not for the first time this evening, she wonders what a man like Trevor sees in a woman like Alice, a woman whose nose bends at the tip and whose cheeks engulf her small eyes. She is a good mother, Jane thinks, but a hostile woman.

Allen removes his hand from Jane's manicured fingers and grabs 63 two more beers from the outdoor cooler. Under the white container lid, the bottles float in tepid water, their labels peeling off like dead skin. He searches for lime wedges, and grows frustrated in the dim light. He turns and knocks on the window, but Jane calls out and shakes her head. The limes are in the kitchen—he is too lazy to go retrieve them. Trevor won't mind. He closes the door to the patio and goes back inside, watching a few moths flutter to the light fixture above. Even when they leave the screen door closed, the moths find their way inside. His wife is right: if the bugs will intrude regardless, better to remove the wire mesh entirely. It is too ugly.

Alice tacitly agrees to stay late so that her husband has a good time. He works hard, and, unlike her, has only one close friend in Allen. Trevor is introverted until he drinks, so she takes it upon herself to find new restaurants and outings when things get slow. There are a few dinner reservations and house visits lined up in the coming weeks, but the Mitchells are their closest friends. She doesn't like Jane, but company is company. Like her, Jane is an only child, and both their fathers have died. There is some comfort in their histories, though not much else. Alice is unyielding, hardworking, disciplined. Jane is carefree, less organized, and equally happy. For the sake of their husbands, they sometimes meet for walks and always exchange gifts for birthdays.

"Wouldn't you rather go on a nice vacation once or twice a year," Jane asks, twirling the stem of her champagne glass, "than buy a cabin—a damn *cabin!*—that doesn't let you go anywhere else and forces you to spend money on repairs and upkeep?"

Alice looks at her watch, a Timex purchased on sale. She realizes that Allen must have gotten a fairly big raise at work. She wonders what it means to go from regional manager to vice president at General Electric. She dislikes the Mitchells for this arrogance; it was typical of them to make it hard to say congratulations. They bragged of their own successes, preventing the nice evening from speaking for itself. "Wouldn't you rather go to Paris, London, Tokyo?" She wants to reply with the frankness that a question like that deserves: of course she'd rather travel! Of course she'd rather have a cabin in the woods! For her and her husband, it isn't a matter of preference. It is a matter of having the opportunity for preference. But, to at once challenge Jane and keep up their façade, she tells her that she'd rather have a cabin. Because if the Mitchells invited them for a weekend, they would be able to go. She thinks to add that they should make sure to have a guest bedroom, but that's a little too on the nose. Besides, she doesn't actually want to go on vacation with the Mitchells.

Allen decides not to hold Jane's hand when he sits back down. She brought up the new house, even though he told her to wait for another night. He genuinely wants to know the Jacksons' opinion, but this is too much. They held a dinner party to celebrate, and his wife just suggested the extent of his new salary. It is a significant raise, he thinks, but not an unexpected one. His boss told him to be proud of the promotion, of the achievement. To mark the occasion more permanently, he already bought a new grill, a Weber, the expensive kind with six burners. He understands that a second house is so much more than a grill, almost like having another child. He can see Alice growing uncomfortable. He spies the straightening of her spine, the smoothing of her dress across her lap.

Jane doesn't know why she brought up the new house. She often compares drinking to getting in the pool: she's cold for a moment and then warm all over. She knows that she shouldn't have said anything, and that Allen specifically warned her of this, but Alice was sitting there, smugly, making her silent criticisms. Soon, Jane knows, Alice will make a comment that unnerves them all. So there is something satisfying about upsetting her, about turning the table, even if it is too easy, even if tomorrow she will regret embarrassing herself. She can never point to the exact moment in the night when Alice spoils the fun, but like the light outside, there is a slow change in color, from a warm yellow to a cold black, until the only sources of light are the individual flashes from fireflies: Trevor, Allen, and her. And though she doesn't know how it got to be so dark, she knows who is responsible.

Trevor is surprised by his happiness for Allen. On some level, he feels that he, too, has been given a promotion, though on what merit he cannot determine. Maybe for being a good friend. Maybe for pretending that he doesn't know his wife hates the Mitchells. Alice says she only hates Jane because of her coyness, but he knows the truth: his wife hates the successes of others. Hate, he acknowledges, is too strong a word, but he likes to deal in extremes. It is why he always drinks too much, works too hard, angers too easily; why he was the best linebacker in high school and college, while simultaneously at risk for losing his scholarship; why he has only one very good friend.

"Well, we were discussing, you know, the *issue* again last week," Alice says, placing her hand on her husband's leg and noticing the tiniest stain just below his knee.

"Babe, not now," Trevor says. "And it's not an 'issue.'"

"No, no. I want to know what they think. What do you think *now* about us having another baby?"

"Well," says Jane.

"Oh," says Allen.

Jane wants to know why she has had this conversation three times in two years. Twice on Alice's birthday, and once on a dinner date. There is no more she can say, but so much more she feels she must: Alice and Trevor do not have enough money; their marriage seems just stable enough to maintain the status quo; their two kids will be out of the house in fewer than ten years. Why would they start over now? Deep down, she knows that this has nothing to do with children. For Alice, children, and any other topic pulled from an imaginary catalogue she might call "Family," are but an excuse to have a conversation with others, a dialogue so that she feels present and acknowledged. Jane's mother, a psychiatrist, told her so during a visit a few months ago. Her mother has many theories about many people, but this one is particularly insightful. Jane has mentioned this to Allen in passing only once, worried that her mother will come across worse than Alice. Tomorrow—and she hopes she will remember the precise way to say it—her husband will learn more of what she really thinks of Alice Jackson. She will say that Alice ruins these dinners with her questions, suffocating conversation with a thick blanket of too-personal topics, all under the guise of lighthearted intimacy. She will try to speak without hyperbole, to restrain herself as best she can, out of respect for Trevor. But Alice has embarrassed herself tonight, far more than her own comment, however calculated, about a new house. Alice talks as though her family inhabits a filing cabinet, color coded by age and sex. These are not issues for the company of others; they are issues for—a therapist.

Allen makes an effort not to look amused, taking as many sips of his beer as he can manage. Trevor, he now remembers, warned him on a recent run that Alice might make a fool of herself: "When she asks, *if* she asks, say something about the kids being out of the house in a few years. Don't mention money. Never mention that." Allen promised that he would stick to the script. He thinks the Jacksons certainly *could* have another baby, but something has stayed with him since that conversation. He was sure he heard a tremor in his friend's voice, one that betrayed a great resistance to the notion of renewed parenthood. It was an almost biological response, and if Trevor had not already had two children, Allen would question his ability to conceive at all.

Trevor had once been so adamant about having kids, about becoming **67** a schoolteacher. Allen knows that these troubles stem from a common source: the Jackson marriage, two people deeply at odds with each other. Through his wife, he has learned that Alice is happy as a mother, just trying to get through the days with her slightly boring husband. But Trevor, living under the same roof, seems caught in a long-lived jet lag, fatigued by something without remedy. "A kid can't solve problems. It only adds more," Trevor told him.

Trevor feels himself loosening up, caring a little less about his wife's behavior. He knows it's the alcohol, and for a fleeting moment he wonders how he will be able to drive home. It is not so much a matter of falling asleep behind the wheel, or even feeling dizzy or light-headed. He is simply not meant to drive this evening, to return home, but he will anyway, because he has made the trip before under worse circumstances and influences. He is almost finished his beer and knows that the time has come for another. He steps outside onto the patio and lifts the lid of the cooler. They are drinking his favorite beer tonight, a grapefruit IPA, which means his friend bought it specifically for him. How nice, he thinks—who would not want to promote this man, who hosts these parties, spends so much money on his friends, and asks for little in return? Only his wife would object, out of envy.

"Maybe we can save this conversation for a different time," Allen proposes.

"You're right. Let's change the subject," Alice replies.

Alice doesn't want another baby. She frustrates herself and puts her marriage and friendships on edge, for—she can't identify an immediate purpose. It just seems like the right way to fill the gap, like when she cuts the line at the store because the person in front of her is distracted and won't notice. She mentioned getting pregnant last week with her husband, just so that they could talk about *something*. She could not

68   see his face as he nodded uneasily, his fingers fumbling with the laces of his sneakers. She picked that moment deliberately, so Trevor would have something to think and talk about on his run. She knows he tells Allen all the details of their relationship, the details the way he sees them, those things she would never confide in Jane. She brought up a topic, serious-seeming—a baby—because they have become a couple that remains silent at dinner, allowing their children to explain every thought in their heads, as though the things they have to say are more meaningful and therefore worthier of conversation. She can't imagine what gets discussed in the Mitchell house, but they are the more cerebral couple: Allen and Jane both read the same books, watch the same shows, finish each other's thoughts. Alice is not jealous, however. She tries to keep up, but Jane reads too much fiction. She sees her mouth in the reflection of her glass, her lips curling upward: the Mitchells read fiction because their lives need to be thrown into relief.

Jane tries to mention a new show that she and Allen are watching, a documentary series about a murder, but she remembers that Trevor does not watch television in the way that they do. He watches basketball and football, at the professional and college level, and sometimes pays attention to the news, which he watches because, she assumes, he feels that's what a person *should* do. She thinks he could have been a sports announcer, instead of a gym teacher. He has managed to stay fit, and despite filling out in the middle, he has never lost that look of a tight end. She wishes her own husband dressed like a commentator. He likes nice things (look at the grill he just bought), but his taste in clothes upsets her. Tonight Alice made a comment about his shirt not matching his jacket, a comment she could not disagree with, no matter its rudeness. Next week she will pick out what he wears to dinner when they all go out to celebrate Trevor's birthday. She should remember to arrange for the babysitter and to buy a gift, one that Allen will suggest. She is not looking forward to the dinner, because the Jackson children will be there. They are nine and ten years old, the age when chatting with adults suddenly becomes appealing. She herself just had her second baby a few months ago, and her first two years before that, so she knows her children and the Jacksons will not be friends. This is, of course, only true if Alice does not get pregnant again—though, who knows? By then, maybe they will have moved away or found new best friends.

Allen wonders how many beers are left the cooler; he worries that Trevor has had too much to drink. Not too much to drink given his height and weight, but too much to drink to drive home safely. Trevor can be reckless at parties, and if he tries to stop him from driving, there will be an argument and Trevor will win. His friend will yell, threaten to wake the neighbors in the houses next door, and he will shake his head and close the front door, disappointed that it should always come to this. When Trevor drinks, he changes into a different person, no less likeable—possibly more likeable—but altogether different. More abrasive and intrusive. His size becomes apparent, because he becomes physical, harder to overlook. Alice, Allen has noticed, welcomes the difference, encourages it even, perhaps because the drunk Trevor becomes more the man she wishes he were: open and sociable, brutish and assertive. He would never tell that to Jane; he would never give her a reason to dislike Alice. He appreciates their friendship, admires it, because it makes these parties and dinners so much better. In truth, he has never understood how the two women get along. A few years ago he asked Trevor how they would manage with two wives so fundamentally different from each other. Trevor said that women could surprise you.

"Any new crazy students, Mr. Jackson?" Jane asks.

Trevor smiles. He looks at Jane with appreciation, as sincerely as possible, though the beers have relaxed the muscles in his face. No one in the world—at least, no one he can name—appreciates his job as a teacher more than she does. At every meal, she asks about the students and the football team. It was Jane who saw when his name appeared in the local paper, who knew when the team had amassed a record number of points for their division, who attended the ceremony when he won an award for coaching. Allen, he admits, also supports him in this way, but for him there is a certain expectation. Jane, as far as he can tell, does not even like sports. She simply cares about him as a friend, as a good person, the kind of person Allen deserves.

Alice refills her glass, disappointed that the bubbles fail to spill over the rim. Does each sip of champagne honor Allen? She digs her feet into the shag carpet and stretches her legs forward. They have been at the Mitchells' house for almost five hours, and her husband has spoken about school too many times to count. She loves that he is a teacher, that he teaches students how to run, how to hit, how to throw a ball. But it's not as if Allen has nothing to talk about. Clearly he has stories of his own, stories of success worth celebrating with dinner parties. She does not want to hear about management at General Electric or Jane's work as a hospital administrator, but she knows that either topic is what they *should* be discussing. She is wearing nice shoes and drinking champagne. School is a topic that she hears about every day from her children. In time, the Mitchells will come to agree with her, when their own children ride the bus each morning. And, she thinks, they will wish they had spent these moments, moments of peace that come too infrequently, talking about something else.

"Did you hear about—well, I'm sure you know about it—but did you hear about that teacher at Ammons?" asks Allen.

"Oh, you know I hate that stuff," Jane replies.

"How old did they say the girl was?"

Jane watches Alice purse her lips. This has happened before, though she has never been too sure of the implications. Whenever a school scandal is brought up, Alice tries to redirect the conversation, as though she and Trevor are somehow involved. It must be a fear of hers, Jane thinks, that Trevor will have an affair with a female student and leave her alone to take care of their family. Jane's own fears are far different. She worries constantly of getting fired, about making an error that makes her look less competent than her peers. She waited weeks before announcing her second pregnancy despite the tightness of her clothes, her more measured gait. It was a silly thing to worry about, because there were so many laws to protect her. But, to her disappointment, she has become far more self-conscious since her second pregnancy. Since that second birth, there has been a change in the way she moves, in the way she handles things, in the way she functions in their little world. She is now more grounded, more stable, but she wants to feel powerful again, carefree, like she can do anything at a moment's notice. She wants the added weight in her hips to fall away with a single stomp of her foot. "You just don't want responsibilities," her mother said. "You're describing youth, being young."

Alice tries hard not to think about these scandals at schools. Trevor would never do such a thing, would never think of doing such a thing, but still she worries. She worries more about what a young girl might say than what an older man might do. Her husband is exactly the kind of teacher that she would have found alluring as a high school student: tall, strong, married with children. Teenagers, she thinks, are not drawn immediately to people or physical features; they are drawn to ideas that lead to mistakes. She has overheard her husband and Allen discussing a teacher they once found attractive, a teacher with whom Trevor now works. The woman is no longer young enough to be the object of students' fantasies, and Alice has difficulty placing her in an attractive light at any age. It was merely the idea of sleeping with a teacher that enticed Trevor and Allen 20 years ago. When she closes her eyes, she imagines a young girl, with breasts just large enough to be called breasts, looking at her husband and concocting a simple lie, the type of lie that can end a family, a marriage, your place in the community.

Allen holds Jane's hand once more, stroking the back of her thumb with his own. Her skin is always softer than his, no matter how much of her moisturizer he borrows. For many years, he assumed that this was a difference between men and women, that men have rough hands and women soft ones. But for work he has met women with hands rougher than his own. He laces his fingers with Jane's, tucking his thumb inside and stroking the inside of this makeshift pocket, her palm. How much longer will Trevor and Alice stay? He lets go of Jane's hand and moves his arm slowly, cautiously, to her back, careful not to distract her while she speaks. He makes figure eights against her dress with his forefinger, before dragging his hand up to her neck where he lightly pinches her nape. He hears a lilt in Jane's voice when he tickles her, though she gives no indication for him to stop. He hopes the Jacksons decide to leave.

"Listen to that thunder!" Trevor says. "The storm is coming after all. Better bring those beers inside."

"You just want an excuse for another drink," Alice replies.

"So what?"

"I'll grab you a lime," says Jane.

"I'll help you," says Allen.

Trevor pulls back the screen door and steps outside. He feels the wind picking up, shaking the vinyl cover of Allen's new grill. It's a large grill, sturdy, one that he would like to own himself. He picks up the cooler with both hands, more quickly than he should, and the water inside sloshes over the edge and onto his pants. That's alright, he thinks. Better than a bottle of wine! He walks back through the screen door and closes it behind him, cradling the container awkwardly in his arms. He realizes that he should drain the water out in the grass, so

he opens the screen door once more, steps down the brick steps, and 73
unplugs the white plastic spout. The water rushes out quickly, and
eventually he tilts the container to let out the final drops. There are
two more beers left: one for him and one for Allen. They will try to get
him to stop drinking, but it's September. He needs to enjoy these last
days of summer. Let him have his fun.

Alice watches Trevor through the window, fumbling with the cooler
like a little boy carrying something too big for his body. He has had too
much to drink. Here is the proof: this wetness on his pants, so much
wetness that in any other circumstance one would assume he poured
water on himself intentionally, or even more embarrassing...How much
longer will they stay? She checks her watch. It is close to midnight;
they have been here longer than any other time, longer even than the
time when Trevor passed out on the couch. She wonders if her husband
drinks because that is what people do at parties like this, or because he
needs to. The only test would be for Allen and Jane to have a dinner
party every day. Then she could keep track of his behavior with a mental
checklist, gauging his interactions with others, his sips of beer.

"Do you think they'll leave sometime soon?" Allen asks.

"Shh, a minute. I'm listening to the monitor," says Jane.

"I told you we could have kept the babysitter longer."

"It was late, and she shouldn't have to stay just because of them."

"Well, what about us? What about, you know?"

Allen reaches over Jane's shoulder and pulls the monitor from
her ear. He wraps his hand around her waist, pulling her body against
his own. He feels the warmth between them, that arousal, the end of
the night arriving on cue. How many years has he known her? She
has had just enough to drink, and he knows what comes next. Why
has it become so hard to be parents and lovers? There are two babies
upstairs, each a part of him, like limbs that ache and stir, parts of him

that keep him from sleeping. He often thinks of how simple they are, how animalistic: they eat; they sleep; they cry. He and Jane have joked about the way children play in the park, shouting out half-commands, falling over, hurting themselves. "They look drunk," Jane said last week. He holds the monitor close to his ear, waiting for the rise and fall of breath. There is always a moment of panic when he or Jane thinks to run upstairs or into the next room, but if they wait long enough, the monitor will produce that sign of life, and they will know that all is well. Suddenly he hears music. He lets go of Jane, and they walk towards the living room. Trevor is swaying with Alice, who laughs and tries to keep his big shoes off her bare toes.

"I'm sorry, he said he wanted music!" says Alice.

Jane curls her arm around Allen's neck. She closes her eyes. This, she thinks, is what the night needed. A little night music! She smiles to herself. They are listening to an album she left in the stereo, an old CD she found at a yard sale. She hears the jazz, the buzz of the woman's voice, the thrum of fingers against the wooden bass. Caramel, she thinks. Rich, dark sugar swirling in the bottom of a pan. She can almost smell it. "I love you," Allen whispers in her ear.

"Who is singing, Jane?" Alice asks.

"Her name is Etta Jones."

"Etta James, you mean."

"No, Etta James sings 'At Last.' This is Etta Jones. She's less known. Here, listen to this."

Jane pulls away from her husband and picks up the remote from the table. She bites her lip and changes the song. No, she thinks, this one is too fast. She can't remember the title or any of the lyrics. She never used to be this aware of alcohol, this conscious of a change in body temperature. She feels little bursts of heat rising under her skin, trapped pockets of warm air that she can't let out even as she presses against her face. She sees herself drinking, being drunk, as though there are two versions of her, the one changing the music with clicks of the remote and the one thinking of how difficult it is to make these tiny clicks. At what point should she stop drinking? Are there still rules for quantity, even after breastfeeding? No, there are no more rules besides those she sets for herself. She flips through the album, listening to each track for some thirty seconds. Alice sits down on the couch and sighs at the brief disruption in the music. It wouldn't be a proper party if she didn't give Alice something to complain about. But she will win this exchange, and the wait will have been worth it. Finally, she finds it—she hears the piano twinkling.

"This one. Listen to this one."

Trevor has not heard the song before, but trusts Jane's taste in music. She has an ear for this sort of thing, more than Allen or his own wife. They have all gone to the theater before, and Jane is always the one who explains the backstory, why something is important, why they should be more appreciative than they are. She could have been a teacher, Trevor thinks. The song is beautiful; he can hear it now. What a voice this woman—not Etta James—had. He takes another sip of his beer, frowning at the flat taste. Alice used to be a singer, he remembers. In college, he met many women who sang—in the chorus, onstage—but Alice was different. She sang because she wanted to, not because she needed to be heard and wanted others to listen. She used to sing to their kids; she used to sing, softly, after they had sex and he would play with her hair.

"You're not gonna join me for this one?" Trevor asks.

"Maybe in a minute. I feel woozy," Alice answers.

"I won't leave you like that!" Allen jokes.

Jane sits down on the couch next to Alice, pleased that the song is as lovely as she remembers. She laughs when her husband puts his arm behind Trevor's back, so that they dance together like a couple. She looks at Alice and catches her smiling. They nod at each other in a silent exchange, a mutual understanding that this closeness between their husbands, formed through childhood, is why they are still up, though it's already past midnight. Trevor is the bigger man in the embrace, though it's unclear which one of them, if either, is leading. Her husband leans against Trevor for support, a man propped against a wall. Trevor, despite having drunk the most, is now in control. His hand rests on the back of Allen's head. How funny, Jane thinks, that she has seen him throw her husband into the pool with relative ease. They are such different sizes, such different people. Her mother once told her to watch out for Trevor Jackson. She would never do such a thing—she isn't that kind of person. What would an affair look like, sound like? "Half my patients have had affairs," her mother told her, "and none of them thought they ever would." A few years ago, it would have been unthinkable, but now she knows that moments do arise when a simple look or remark can mean so much more at thirty-five than it did at twenty-five. At twenty-five, everyone made those remarks, those flirtations, because that was what you did to show the world who you were becoming, who you would become. But now, she has lost the ability to hide behind herself. She is a mother. Her first child tells her to sit, to come, to read a book. Alcohol brings back that confidence for an hour until she remembers the truth; she wishes she could live her life two drinks in.

Alice hangs her head over her lap. She hopes that if she pretends to fall asleep, the night will end and she can return home to pay the babysitter who has earned too much money for a single night. But no one notices her. She looks up at the dancing, if that is the right word. Her husband is whispering in Allen's ear, probably encouraging him to get to sleep. She knows that her eyes have widened, that her cheeks are stretched upward, that she feels something light inside, as though the night has decided to restart itself. It is the music, the alcohol, the end of a long day. She danced with Trevor for the first time in many months. But why does it feel like one dance can brighten the color of the walls, exaggerate the tickle of champagne bubbles against her upper lip? She loves this feeling, this lightness, more than anything else. Trevor will be thirty-six years old next week. They have been married for ten years, a decade. And, like everyone told her on her wedding day, the years really do start to go by faster. She tells herself not be so sappy. She knows that wine and champagne have given only to take away; the happiness is false, and short. She has compared this buzz to when she nursed her children, to when they hug her, to when she sees them sing in the choir. Those feelings are the pure thing. Tonight she has danced and laughed under the spell of an industry.

"'Make your mark for your friends to see. But when you need more than company, don't go to strangers. Come on to me.' God, I just love that," says Jane, squeezing Alice's hand.

"Yes, I heard it. Thank you for playing the song," Alice replies, smiling.

Allen smells Trevor's deodorant. It is crisp, wintry, like the middle of a forest. "Just another minute," he wants to say. The room spins and spins around him, and he looks for his wife. She is across the room, a world away, though he can number the steps between them. He hopes she will not forgo their plans for later. The night and the thunderstorm, music, and conversation have suddenly become too much. He needs to separate the room into segments before he can continue: Alice sits on the couch, smiling to herself, aglow; Jane is next to her, laughing at him and his inability to stand up straight; the music plays over his ears, under his feet; and Trevor, his friend, his brother, holds him because he can no longer hold himself. He tells himself to focus, to count the

78 beats in the music. Why did Alice have to sit down on the couch? He saw the way the Jacksons danced, the way they stumbled together. Don't give up hope! Suddenly he feels a racing against his skin. It is Trevor's heart, beating faster than the music, chasing something that will not be outpaced. He worries that Trevor will fall over, but there is no change in their balance. They are still moving, turning in place.

Trevor strokes the back of Allen's head, brushing against the grain of his hairline. Allen is suddenly very drunk, much drunker than any of them conceived. He realizes that if he steps away, even for a brief pause, Allen will topple over, like a newly felled tree. He remembers the water at the bottom of his shirt, his soaked pants. Surely Allen can feel this dampness against his own clothes. Trevor sways to the music, to the song chosen by Jane, whispering in Allen's ear whatever words come to mind. In this embrace, Allen is the vulnerable one, the one ready to collapse, the one lost in drunken reverie. There is an intimacy between them, far greater than the one Trevor has imagined during their runs and conversations at dinner. He is so small, Trevor thinks. Like a kid who has come running. Allen says nothing, but Trevor understands that this is merely part of the dance. His heart begins to race, at first arhythmically to the music, then in double-time. He thinks of an agility drill, how his heart punches against his chest the way two cleats shuffle up and down against the ground. Can Allen feel it? They have never been so close to one another. He looks down, but Allen's eyes are closed, his face clean-shaven and relaxed. He wants his friend to smile, to give some indication that this dance will continue, if not now, then later, when they can acknowledge the current traveling between them, this current they have avoided for years. The music fades. He feels something sink. Tomorrow, he realizes, they will wake up as though nothing has happened.

Allen waits for the music to restart, but Jane has already skipped

through every track. He feels helpless, naked, though Trevor continues 79
to turn them around on the floor. Here is another lull. But no, something
has changed. The atmosphere isn't the same—this is nothing like a
quiet lunch. He pushes Trevor away with a nudge, feeling the cushion
of flesh against his knuckles. Did that hurt him? But Trevor is a strong
man, capable of picking him up and tossing him in the pool. He looks
up. Will Trevor retaliate and shove him backward, harder, so his head
hits the ground with a thud? But Trevor has already returned to his
beer. Allen raises his chest.

Alice takes the music stopping as an invitation to leave. It seems
that Trevor will not notice her many sighs, the glances at her watch, the
quiet pleas she makes with her eyes. She rises from her seat and slips
back into her shoes. She will offer to drive, and her husband will, of
course, refuse. Tonight he has behaved differently, and it will take her
some time tomorrow to sort everything out. Instead of rowdy, he has
been calm, subdued in a way she doesn't recognize. Maybe it was the
mixture of champagne, whiskey, and beer, a cocktail that has tampered
with his constitution. Maybe he feels what she felt for that short instant
on the couch. She has also seen another side of Allen, the drunk and
helpless side. He needs to go lie down and fall asleep, she thinks. He
has had a long day.

Jane lets the Jacksons out of the house, closing the door behind
them with a flick of her wrist and swish of her hair. She turns around
and walks back into the living room. Her husband is lying on the couch,
staring at the ceiling. She watches his eyes widen and shift back and
forth under his glasses. "Look who's tired now!" she says. No more
after-party fun for them then. It was unlike him to make plans and not
follow through, but he, like she, is exhausted. There is always tomorrow
for more celebration in the privacy and comfort of their bedroom. It will
be Saturday, which means that she will wake up, still early because of

80 her babies, and nap throughout the day when the nanny comes.

"Goodnight," says Jane. "I love you."

Allen closes his eyes without replying, pretending to be asleep. Those words, simple ones spoken thousands of times per day, are different tonight. Tonight they were whispered by someone else. ✄

"Don't Go to Strangers" is Matthew Jeffrey Vegari's first fiction in print.

THE GARDEN OF EARTHLY DELIGHTS

TROY JOLLIMORE

Because order matters: breakfast, then lunch,
then dinner, dessert following the main course;
the orgasm, yes, but the foreplay before;
old age, yes, but first youth:
Dante's *Divine Comedy* only considered
a "comedy" in so far as it ends
in Paradise, having first given us
a grand tour of the Inferno and then
Purgatory, as methodical if not
quite so easy as A, B, C;
so that, when we look at Bosch's *Garden*
of Earthly Delights, it matters whether
we read it, as readers of English will tend to,
from left to right, beginning in Paradise,
where Dante's masterpiece ends,
then passing through that ebullient garden
bursting with the planet's abundance of pleasures
on the way to that culminating, grotesque,
and, one assumes, irrevocable final
destination, the grim fate that we, in Dante,
climb out of—we, that is, the readers,
the viewers, the detached, impartial observers,
carrying the passports that permit us safe passage
into and out of these unearthly zones,
and not, by any means, the internees,
those who have been granted, against their will

82 and without their asking (though Dante's Virgil
would have disagreed, insisting that they did,
in effect, ask for this, that they did indeed will it)
permanent residence status—or whether,
in fact, we read it in some other way,
as, for example, presenting these
three states of being suspended
before us all at once, as if,
at any moment, we might slip partially
or even completely into any one of them,
or, for that matter, as if at any moment,
an elemental intrusion from hell or paradise
might erupt, without warning, into our lives—
so that the story is not a tale of causation
(sin leads to hell, light to darkness, delight
to damnation) but rather a manner of grasping
the complexity of our existence, how things
that are opposite, if they do not attract,
at the very least coexist, taking place
in one and the same moment, the disparate
constituents of human life that do not,
as one might have expected, when brought into contact,
annihilate one another, but instead,
by the very force of their contrast, heighten
and strengthen each other. What, other than evil,
could make virtue shine so bright? What, other than
purity and naïve hope, could entice
corruption and despair into bursting forth
to appear so nakedly as what they are?

Because order matters, yes; but our lives
are not orderly. And art, precisely
because it is, feels at times like a mere
detached imitation, yet can also feel
as if it were more like life than life
itself. Which is why, one assumes, we are drawn,
again and again, to the place where the picture
hangs, to stand in its presence, as if
it were only in those moments that we lived.

But we come from elsewhere, and we go elsewhere
when we are done with our looking. That they
are *earthly* delights, indeed, reminds us
that Dante's *Commedia*, too, begins
not in hell but on earth: that famous dark wood,
not a garden of delights, not at all, but a kind
of garden nevertheless, and that
an arrival in Paradise might well take
the form, as in that remarkable final
shot of Tarkovsky's *Solaris*, of
a return to Earth, a real Earth or
a reconstructed Earth, an imagined
garden or a painted garden, or simply
the garden where you were born. The leafy
globe, perhaps, that we see when the triptych
is closed. It is the earth that is ours,
and Dante's cosmic love, though it moves
the stars that track their paths through their skies,
is a leafy thing, a fleshly thing,
a thing of the soil, a thing that demands

84   to be lived out on this surface, on the face
of this terrestrial sphere, this local
unheavenly orb, this, our planet,
our neighborhood, if, that
is to say, it is to be lived at all.

Troy Jollimore is the award-winning author of three books of poetry, including Syllabus of Errors *(Princeton University Press), and three books of philosophy. His essay "Shawn's Late Night" was published in Issue No. 111.*

E IS FOR EDWARD
WHO WAS NOT REALLY THERE

GLEN DAVID GOLD

—E is for Edward who was not really there—

In 2001, shortly after Edward Gorey's death, I went to Gotham Book Mart on West 47ᵗʰ Street in Manhattan. Gotham, which represented Gorey's estate, was a throwback to the Beats, sort of a narrower, taller version of City Lights Bookstore, with secret rooms, momentary art exhibitions, and even a residence hidden away inside. The woman who greeted me was the opposite of an Edward Gorey character, sunny and friendly, with something of a 1960s persona, so much so that a portrait of her by R. Crumb decorated her workspace.

86   I was there to inquire about original artwork, so she let me down easy: people had been obsessed with Gorey's work since the 1950s. Anything that made it my way would be what the inner circle had already rejected. And they didn't reject much. So that day, sorry, there was nothing.

She had, however, a tantalizing story. After Gorey passed away, she had gone to his house to catalogue its holdings, and when she removed work from a filing cabinet she had found secreted therein a treasure trove of previously unknown pages. I am an art collector by nature, and a fiction writer, so every description of every unknown haul becomes immediately in the yeast of my imagination the Ark of the Covenant reflected off the mirrors of Aladdin's cave. Let's just say there was unpublished stuff, and I left Gotham Book Mart knowing that soon it would be available.

Gorey himself was a collector, with a collector's personality, having a certain emotional detachment from people. By all accounts he was hyper-intelligent and distant, not so much reserved as uninterested, with, not surprisingly, a cat's level of affection. He collected housecats and rings and iron scraps and sea shells and art, but mostly what he collected were bits of bling that added up to a self.

What I mean by that, and what is carefully catalogued in Mark Dery's excellent new biography, *Born to Be Posthumous*, is that Gorey seems to have known from birth who he was. But it did take him a few years to assemble the requisite presentation of self for the outside world. Coming from the same human clay as the rest of us, he evolved into a lanky, bearded, fur-coat-and-high-tops dry wit. In the Tarot deck, he was a Major Arcana figure: The Author, who made pithy remarks at the edge of the crowd, prowling away before the end of the party to read or to watch soap operas while he worked.

About that work: when I was about nine years old, I complained of

being bored and my parents' friend Mark handed me a copy of *Amphigorey*, 87
the then newly published collection of his work. Deep within it was a
children's primer, *The Gashlycrumb Tinies*, in which twenty-six children
suffer cruel and yet hilarious deaths expressed through rhyme: "A is
for Amy who fell down the stairs/ B is for Basil assaulted by bears."
Each was memorialized with a dreary single panel of ruthlessly specific
crosshatching and textures suggesting twilight gloom interrupted only
by the form of the wan, tiny victim about to be dispatched.

Mark pointed to this one: "N is for Neville who died of ennui,"
and he said, "This is you."

Never have I so quickly understood an illustration and never have
I felt so well understood in return. I have been a professional writer
for twenty years and I have been explaining my responses to books for
fifty, and yet I still can't do a full exegesis on why this panel spoke to
me so much. Part of me—and all of Gorey, I think—would be fine to
leave it there, but as with most things we love, we need to tear them
to shreds to see what they, y'know, *mean*, and so here we are, getting
out the eviscerating shears to have a go at the creator's life for signs
of thematic resonance.

If you are the type of person who wants to know about artists,
upon discovering Gorey, you probably learned the same outlines I did:
no, he wasn't an Edwardian fop but a Midwestern eccentric who left
the country but once (a trip to Scotland). He was probably gay but
never had sex with anyone. He lived early on with many cats in a tiny
place in Manhattan, illustrating weird books (his own and others') and
attending nearly every performance of every ballet choreographed by
Balanchine. He managed during that period to continue not to have
sex. Upon Balanchine's death in 1983, he moved to Cape Cod, where
he lived in a decaying sea captain's house, still writing and drawing
among cats, eating in the same café every day, continuing his witty

but distant banter with acquaintances, and replacing Balanchine with TV shows like *Buffy the Vampire Slayer*. Still, no sex. Then, in 2000, he died while a workman was trying to fix his TV remote. The end.

If you turn to this biography to get more dirt, I've got some unsurprising news for you: there isn't any. Dery is a fine writer and he has done a superb job shaking every tree, taking a flashlight across every fen and bog, opening every cellar and attic—and there's nothing. He has psychologically and literarily and deconstructionist-ly banged on every piece of work like a piñata and *nothing* has come out.

However, I'm not saying reading the book is anything other than a rewarding experience. "Nothing" is a very Edward Gorey prize to win. Gorey certainly cherished "nothing" himself, at least as an ideal if not a description of his totality of affection. Dery captures these feelings, beginning with the title of his lovely piece of Gorey-ana. If you were born to be posthumous, then all that in-between stuff is just happenstance. Clever.

What's truly weird, as this biography makes plain, is that Gorey had no wrong turns nor false starts. He didn't try at first to be a merchant seaman nor a bass guitarist. There were no laudanum binges nor youthful orgies where the men stripped down to their spats. As soon as he could draw, he drew funny little men in fur coats (no detours into social realism or plein air landscapes) and then he just kept doing it. Even in childhood, he seems like a tiny Edward Gorey, eyes rolling with an *oh bother* attitude. As he said, "I lead a dreary life.... My interests are solitary, I don't do anything."[1]

This is good for us, his audience, in that beginning with his college work, his storytelling—his pictures and his words together—is glorious,

---

1 *Mark Dery,* Born to be Posthumous: The Eccentric Life and Mysterious Genius of Edward Gorey *(Little, Brown and Company, 2018) p. 153*

E IS FOR EDWARD WHO WAS NOT REALLY THERE

executed with a visionary's control from his layouts to his mysteriously 89
engaging font. And without any of that insidious boning to take up the
attention of his daily life, there ends up being an incredible amount of
work to read. Some better than others, but all instantly recognizable.
Even the least of his books has something to recommend it.

But it's also problematic for the biographer. Gorey seems to have had
no trauma, no setbacks, no accidents, no real struggle, no heartbreak—

Well, that's not exactly true. He very possibly had sex with someone
once and then decided the whole rigmarole wasn't worth it. There were
flirtations to be sure, and Dery admirably chases down every possible
encounter the way scholars perform forensics on dubious Shakespeare
verse for signs of authenticity. It's important to get the specifics of
desire right, and Dery gets as close as maybe anyone can with this
footnote: "Gorey was a professed asexual whose social presentation
of self was stereotypically gay and whose only sexual experiences, as
far as we know, were with members of the same sex."

That's a whole lot of words to describe what is basically a shrug
of the shoulders, a parsing of the "nothing" that might be found about
three millikelvins above absolute zero. But all this absence is intriguing.
Of himself, Gorey often said things like: "There is a strong streak in
me that wishes not to exist and really does not believe I do."[2] We can
learn about him from his opinion of the artist he hated the most: Henry
James. James was another queer writer who would hate to be identified
that way, whose passions are also close to unknown, and whose literary
crimes Dery summarizes as "lunkheaded insistence on explaining things
to death, which kills ambiguity and with it, subtlety, leaving no room
for imaginative participation by the audience."[3]

---

2 *p. 273*

3 *p. 165*

Agreed, but this puts a biographer in a tough spot. Part of his job is to sort out all those ambiguities, to expose every available detail to light. In Gorey's case, the details are tiny. His father left his mother for another woman. He was in the Army (stationed in Utah as a clerk). He went to Harvard, where he roomed with Frank O'Hara and was friends with abstract expressionist Joan Mitchell. (They liked each other but loathed each other's work.) For a recluse, he was in a lot of crowded rooms at times, meeting (or almost meeting) Andrew Sarris, Susan Sontag, Joseph Cornell, William K. Everson, Allegra Kent, Patricia McBride, Maurice Sendak, Charles Addams, Alex Theroux, and Johnny Ryan, but narrowly missing Louise Brooks, if my understanding of the timeline is correct.

For the most part, the drama in the book turns on almost trivial shifts. When an editor who hired him changed houses, he briefly wondered if he would change, too. (Spoiler alert: he did.) Stuff like that. I can see this book sitting on the shelf with the film *How to Draw a Bunny*, which excavates the life of the mysterious artist Ray Johnson, peeling back layers until there's literally nothing left except his desire to make art. Dery sees some of Johnson in Gorey's mail art, as well as traces, if you hold the magnifying glass properly, of the aforementioned Maurice Sendak and Joseph Cornell, as well as Andy Warhol, Samuel Beckett, Gertrude Stein, Louis Feuillade, and Tomi Ungerer.

The appreciation for minutiae does lead to some interesting subtext. There's all kinds of queerness lurking in plain sight here. I hadn't noticed that the distant uncle in *The Hapless Child* is brained by masonry because he's staring at a male statue's shapely buttocks. And there's some anger, too—apparently *The Beastly Baby*, which is about what you think it's about, was inspired by his friend Alison Lurie betraying him by having the audacity to give birth.

A larger revelation, to me at least, was that *The Doubtful Guest*,

Gorey's 1957 masterwork about an otterish creature that moves in **91**
with a family and ruins everything, came out the same year as *The
Cat in the Hat*—they share the same damned setup, more or less. The
Seuss book seems radical at first ("our caretaker is INSANE") but is
ultimately conservative ("let's clean up our mess"). Gorey's, however,
is conservative at first glance (just look at the Edwardian structure
of the illustrations) and then is quite radical. (Nothing is fixed and
the creature is probably going to never leave.) Dery also provides a
Freudian interpretation of *The Doubtful Guest* that is so formfitting
it also resolves the mystery of the thing, which is a bit distressing, so
I won't share it here.

When Gorey's ability to draw faded a bit in the '80s, he turned to
other media, designing the title sequence for PBS's *Mystery* and the
sets for the stage production of *Dracula*. This led to his own producing
of small-scale onstage dramas that Dery finds to be a fruitful career
direction. But as someone who sat through a performance of *English
Soup* at the Storyopolis Gallery in Los Angeles in 1998, I would present
the perhaps minority view that they weren't actually that good. (Look up
the word *oeuthre* for details.) The actors were his neighbors (I believe one
of them was actually Gorey's mailman), and their delivery deliberately
amateurish. The experience was like being at a party where you could
hear every third line of dialogue, the charm of which faded quickly. It
made us, the audience, uncomfortable, as it felt like it was supposed
to mean something but that meaning was withheld from us.

Still, Gorey really was at his best when slinging nonsense that
seemed to have an extra gear, a moment that stuck with you for reasons
you couldn't quite work out. Beyond the macabre stuff, which gives a
laugh and a pleasurable gruesome Halloween frisson, the harder-to-
explain work always operated like some poetry, bypassing the intellect
and going instead for the emotions.

Dery is very good with examining *The West Wing*, one of Gorey's more enigmatic books, a series of textless, silent panels showing tableaux of the interior of a mansion. Some are fairly straightforward, like peeling wallpaper, or a girl sitting pensively on a rug. But most are unsettlingly eerie and inexplicable, a room half-filled with ocean water, a geologic fissure across a hallway floor, an apparition in a window. My hunch is that Gorey had seen *Last Year at Marienbad* and was inspired both by its endless tracking shots of rich interiors and its resolute disruption of the narrative so that you literally couldn't follow it, no matter how hard you tried.

In Gorey's hands, this creates feelings of dread, melancholy, resolve, humor, and, maybe acceptance. The experience of reading it, or at least looking at one image after the other, means you might try to put the pieces together as a narrative, then fail. And yet each new enigma builds toward a kind of world that you can participate in, but never understand. The last image is of a lit candle, tilted and floating. It looks like it's about to be snuffed out. *"The West Wing,"* Gorey said in interviews, "is where you go when you die." So it's a narrative-free narrative about the most meaningful (or meaningless) thing in the world. That sounds about right.

Some two years after my first visit to Gotham Book Mart I decided to see if I could actually buy something. I took the precaution of calling ahead and was told that indeed they had some unseen Gorey to sell. I was given an appointment to meet Gotham's patriarch, Andreas Brown. Brown, who doesn't seem to have been interviewed for the biography, is an eccentric figure. (Of *course* he fucking is.) He seems to be controversial, for reasons I've only heard vague whispers about. Apparently, his logical and literary decisions make as much sense as your average Gorey narrative.

When I was ushered into their brand-new offices he was cordial, happy to meet a new Gorey fan, and easily distracted by any bit of **93** business that might flitter by. I liked him. We beat around the bush for a while, and then he asked if I was interested in perhaps buying some artwork. There was a vault, a literal vault behind him, and he directed a staff member to open it for us to see what illustrations were inside.

A moment later, the staff member appeared at the desk, troubled. The vault was empty.

Brown got up, went to the vault, peered in, and came back. "Why so it is. There's nothing in there. How odd." ✄

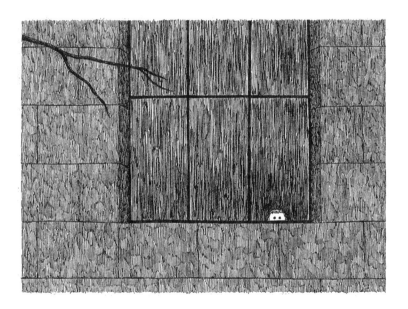

Edward Gorey (American, 1925–2000). Illustration from Gashlycrumb Tinies, *courtesy Pomegranate Communications, Inc. © The Edward Gorey Charitable Trust*

Glen David Gold is the author, most recently, of the memoir I Will Be Complete *(Knopf). He lives in Los Angeles.*

Edward Gorey illustrations are used by arrangement with the Edward Gorey Charitable Trust.

THE ROUGH BEAST TAKES A PAINTING CLASS

ALEXANDRA TEAGUE

*The surface of American society is covered with a layer of
democratic paint, but from time to time one can see the old
aristocratic colours breaking through.*

—Alexis de Tocqueville, *Democracy in America*

The teacher says white is not truly a color,
containing as it does, all wavelengths of visible light.

She says the Rough Beast's claws might be useful later
for scraffito—to scratch back through to what's beneath:

cyan and *magenta; Goldman-Sachs* and *Donald Trump.*
The teacher says *Trump is not a color.* But everyone knows

he's on the wheel between *Versailles-mirror-hall* and *rosebush*
with limp orange petals and a shitstorm of thorns. All the brushes' bristles

are made of his hair. It's hard to keep the paint from clumping.
The Best Color Wheel is segregated into swaths—no way to spin it

like a Twister spinner: *blueviolettangerinecharcoalforesttealyellow.*
No way to step on two colors with the same foot at once.

The teacher says there is no color called *Keep Out,*
although the Beast has seen it. In pointillism, the world

sieves into so many tiny dots—a thousand points of light—
until it's hard to tell which dot amid the swan boat   dot

parasol   dot   lakes with a golfcourse   dot   is democracy.   **95**
She shows battleships dazzle-painted in Cubist camouflage:

black and white angles and stripes like a flotilla of zebras.
This was supposed to confuse torpedoes. She doesn't say

if the lesson shows the limits of deception or imagination.
She arranges a still life to keep everything still: a peacock's

hues simmered down to two glimmering feathers, a skull
resting loudly by a fruitbowl. *No one would eat a Cezanne apple,*

she explains, meaning people want realism more than truth.
Good apples do not complain about the light that hits them.

Alexandra Teague is the author of the novel The Principles Behind Flotation *(Skyhorse) and the forthcoming poetry collection* Or What We Call Desire, *to be published by Persea in May. Her poems appeared in Issue No. 97.*

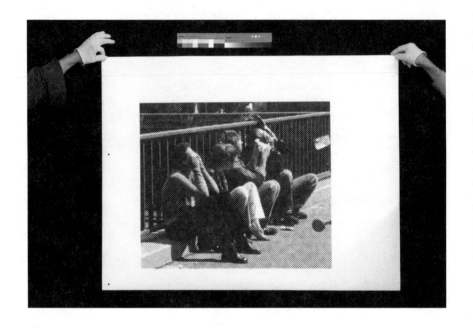

JORDAN KANTOR

Untitled (Eclipse with handlers), 2012
courtesy: Jordan Kantor Studio

ON THE SHELF/ON THE WALL

DEAN RADER & JORDAN KANTOR
IN CONVERSATION

In late 2017, over several months, poet Dean Rader and artist Jordan Kantor sat down for an extended conversation about shared concerns within their respective fields. Meeting regularly in San Francisco's Mission District, where Kantor has a studio, their discussions ranged from artistic homage, originality, and process to questions of accessibility and how poetry and visual art might speak to contemporary politics. Over the course of these conversations, it became clear their ideas about the matrix of art, poetry, and society shed light on important features of their individual practices at mid-career.

Indeed, that time proved to be an interesting year for both. The first major monograph on Kantor's studio practice, *Jordan Kantor: Selected Exhibitions 2006–2016*, was published, covering the decade-plus since he relocated to the Bay Area from New York. Since then, Kantor's work has been exhibited locally at venues as diverse as the San Francisco Museum of Modern Art, the Wattis Institute of Contemporary Art, 871 Fine Arts, and Ratio 3, but that book introduced this conceptually based interdisciplinary art to a wider audience. For his part, Rader saw two books of his poems released in 2017, *Self-Portrait as Wikipedia Entry* (Copper Canyon Press) and *Suture* (Black Lawrence), a collection of sonnets co-written with Simone Muench. The following is a condensed version of Rader and Kantor's discussions.

98

DEAN RADER In one of our first conversations about poetry and painting, you said something I thought was both insightful and ironic. You observed that I am a poet who wants to be on the wall, and you are a painter who wants to be on the shelf. Why the shelf?

JORDAN KANTOR I was trying to express then something of my experience that books go places artworks do not. Artworks, for better or worse, are so obstinately physical, fragile, and logistically difficult. I am interested in how books can compress information into a small, portable, and durable format, which can reach more and more diverse populations than artworks do. The low cost of books compared to unique artworks is key here, too.

But the other half of our exchange was about your interest in being a "poet on the wall." Why the wall?

DR I might say the same thing—an interest in reaching people who would not otherwise see my work. But, beyond that, I am interested in the act of looking at poetry, not just reading it. That might sound like a reversal of what a poet would be expected to say, but to me poetry is as much a visual text as it is a linguistic or verbal text. And so, I'm intrigued by what happens when viewers bring the same set of anticipatory and aesthetic lenses to a poem as they would to a painting. What happens to the experience of interacting with a poem if you are coming to it as though it were a painting?

That leads me to the *Selected Exhibitions* book. There is a fascinating correspondence there between how works appear on the page and how they were shown on the wall of the documented exhibitions. At times, your shows can seem installed in ways that recall book design. For example, the design, the layout, of your 2016 show at the Columbus College of Art and Design looks bookish to me. In fact, as you walk into the exhibition, it seems as though you are looking at the frontispiece of a book. Even the white rectangularity of the wall denotes a title page with its requisite black and white image and citational data. You prepare us for the act of *looking*. Of *reading*. So, I wonder if you have a similar motivation? Or the opposite? Or can the opposite be the same?

JK Yes, when you said you were interested in the act of looking at poetry, I was thinking that the complimentary formulation is absolutely true for me: that I am interested in how visual art can be *read*. On one hand, this can mean that I emphasize the "extra-painterly"—that is, part of the meaning of what I make is elsewhere, in the networks of historical references and in the ongoing artistic conversations my work engages and speaks back to. This approach runs counter to models of art-making that focus on the autonomy and self-containment of the artwork itself, and to the idea that the artwork must hold everything within it.

However, I believe in more diffuse spatial models of meaning. The Columbus exhibition engaged "reading" in much more explicit ways: I planned that exhibition while working on the design of the book in which I knew its documentation was to be ultimately included. Therefore, there was a kind of reversal at work—of making a show for a book as much as documenting a show in a book. One place where this thinking took me was to consider how the design process (which was a collaboration with the great graphic designer Geoff Kaplan) might motivate or guide the installation logics of the exhibition. With this premise in mind, I started to have fun with aspects of the installation that nod to how a page is composed in layout.

But back to your point, what are the stakes of looking at poems?

DR We tend to think of reading as private, whereas we think of viewing or looking as public. Just think about the many assumptions attached to "reading a poem"—all representations connote solitude. But, if a poem is up on a wall, and three or four people are looking

100 at it simultaneously, engaging the poem becomes a public act, a shared act, or more precisely, a hybridized act that is at once both public and private. That's the best of both worlds.

I'm very attracted to the idea of poetry as a common, and there is an historical precedent for this by way of the broadside, and, more recently, through Dada and Surrealism. These poets believed altering the form and structure of a poem was not merely aesthetic but political. Undermining literary form was, at its core, a revolutionary act.

On a smaller level, foregrounding the act of looking at a poem relieves the viewer/reader of the self-imposed anxiety of "understanding" or "comprehending" the poem—what I call "poetry angst." One way I attempt to diffuse that anxiety is by utilizing common visual forms. For example, in *Works & Days*, there

"These poets believed altering the form and structure of a poem was not merely aesthetic but political."

is a poem that parodies the awfulness of a PowerPoint presentation. Another poem appears in the form of bulleted talking points, and another in the form of a pop song. These poems announce themselves visually as well as lexically.

I am often envious of a painting's ability to register an immediate emotional impact on the viewer. We don't necessarily think we have to understand color or shape the way we do with words.

JK While "understanding" might operate differently in the case of the formal attributes of a painting than with the meaning of a word, I do believe that each color, shape, or gesture has a history of prior uses that remains dormant within it, that haunts it when painted, and informs how these aspects are seen and understood. Roland Barthes has a beautiful metaphor for this which I'll have to look up, something like the prior uses of words cling to them like pipe smoke clings to clothing. Painters take advantage of these previous uses and latent meanings to varying degrees, depending on their strategies (or even relative awareness of them). On the other hand, when I think of what makes poetry poetic, I often associate a feeling with how words go together rather than an understanding of why or how they might be comprehended.

DR Well, I would say that the move to abstract and nonrepresentational gestures in painting spirits things out of the realm of denotation. Looking at the painting is not about decoding the canvas. Mark Rothko says, "A painting is not a picture of an experience; it is an experience." Color can be an experience; form or shape can be an experience. Written language can never be only an experience because we use it to talk to a doctor, a teacher, a child, a pastor, a policeman, a coroner. Written language has as its ontology comprehension.

The poet Robert Bly says we have four ears: one in our head,

one in our chest, one in our stomach, and one in our genitals. He claims poets are envious of musicians because music zooms past the head, hangs out in the chest, and then parties in the genitals. Poetry, at least in America, because of how it is taught, tends to lodge in the head. Maybe Neruda gets to the chest and the genitals, but only if he's lucky.

In any case, I think painting hits all three at once.

JK Written language may have as its ontology comprehension, but do you think spoken language operates in the same way?

DR If not the same then similar. Have you ever read a poem or heard a poem spoken in a language you do not understand? It's totally maddening. Even if the poem rhymes, you feel lost. You feel like you are missing something.

JK Yes, however, I believe many people have a similar, maddened response to abstract painting—believing, *contra* Rothko, that they don't have access or can't experience that language. His claim to

102 unmediated experience differentiated from "picturing" something is tied into the rhetoric of Abstract Expressionism, which, by now, we must take with a grain of salt. Perhaps the denotative function of language is more closely related to how representational painting operates, where what is pictured is foregrounded.

DR I agree. In my experience,

corrective) response to what I see as an anti-intellectualism implicit in expecting art to perform emotionally, or expressively.

DR To me, your work is always thinking. Maybe thinking through its emotional register, but always thinking.

JK Thank you. I hope so, because it relates to my process. My studio practice is really broken into a

> *"Perhaps the denotative function of language is more closely related to how representational painting operates, where what is pictured is foregrounded."*

people have learned (or chosen) to sublimate that lack of comprehension of abstract painting to emotion. They don't understand it, but they feel it.

JK I suppose it's precisely that sublimation which frustrates me at times. While I aspire to making work that can be felt as well as analyzed, I'd prefer if my work traffics in ideas as much as emotions. I may have arrived at this position as a kind of contrarian (or

series of discrete phases in which some of these binaries—contrasting thinking with feeling, etc.—are complicated, or at least made less reductive.

There is a nonthinking (perhaps even intuitive) permission that governs the first round of production. The objects that result from that are not yet properly artworks (and some of them never will be). Then, there is a period of editing, in which I try to look at and learn from these objects to build some kind of story—and then nominate some of them to be artworks. This is where my practice comes closest to writing, I think: these arrangements of objects, and formulations of relationships, seem to be like making poems out of individual words. And then, finally, there is another phase—making an exhibition—in which context determines the arrangement, sequence, pacing, and overall experience. This public presentation is vital to the graduation of the objects into artworks. Indeed, it is not by chance that my monograph is organized by exhibitions rather than by sequences of discrete works.

DR For me, I begin a poem because I can't get a line out of my head, or there is a problem I want to solve, or there is something, formally, I want to experiment with. Then, it's just editing and writing and editing and writing and editing and writing. I might go through fifty drafts of a stanza or poem before I think it's ready to be published. So in that sense

there are some similarities with our practices.

However, one thing that distinguishes writing from painting is the element of physical technique. I don't have to be competent at drawing letters, I can just type them.

JK What you say about not getting a line out of your head resonates with me. I sometimes become aware in the studio that I have been talking to myself, usually about what isn't right in a painting. I am constantly gauging myself against an internal standard of how things "should" be in the picture. This is the standard I don't want to question as it is happening, but which I try to contextualize when the object is finished, in terms of how I edit or arrange it with other objects in a show (or on the page of a catalog). For me, there is also another important time of mulling that happens when I am preparing the physical object—like stretching a canvas or gessoing its surface. This is one reason why I do all the handwork of making the object myself.

103

104 **DR** It was fun to watch you stretch a canvas the other day. I don't make my own paper. Or my own ink. Or my own books. The physicality of a book is almost never as auratic as a painting. This leads me to larger questions about preciousness and, further, about beauty. Do you ever think about the presence (or absence) of beauty in your work? I ask because would say that I am suspicious of beauty in my own work to some degree, however, and don't aim for it purposely. I aspire to an artistic project with a degree of cultural critique at its core, and while this certainly doesn't disqualify beauty, I do see beauty in art as markedly susceptible to ideological coop-tion. I realize that sounds cynical and grumpy; I don't mean it that

> *"I aspire to an artistic project with a degree of cultural critique at its core, and while this certainly doesn't disqualify beauty, I do see beauty in art as markedly susceptible to ideological cooption."*

I even want my angry poems to be beautiful, but also because I find beauty in your work, even in your darker, more oblique pieces. I see beauty in your work much the way I see beauty in Manet's. There but not there. Or, rather not obviously there but still there.

JK I am happy to hear people describe the experience of finding beauty in my work. I like beauty and love beautiful paintings. I way. The kind of beauty I hope for in my work is darker and cooler: more like the beauty of math, perhaps. Maybe this gets close to some of the things I find beautiful in Manet? I am interested in this question, however, and wonder what the opposite of beauty is in this context. It doesn't seem like it would be ugliness. What could your angry poems be if not also beautiful?

DR Conventional. Predictable. Lazy. Monotone. I think it's the latter I'm most afraid of. I want my work to sound more than one note; to hit on all registers, like a complex chord. To me the opposite of beauty is not ugliness but complacency. You and I both are drawn to especially rigorous art. Another thing we share is our interest not simply in our predecessors but in quoting or referencing our predecessors.

JK There are many reasons I evoke previous artists, with varying degrees of explicitness, in my work. One reason is to try to enter an ongoing conversation that can happen across space and time. When Manet quotes Velázquez, he is honoring, updating, and contradicting him all at once. At the same time, he is making the past relevant for the present in new ways, and maybe even rewriting history. I am really interested in how Borges formulates this phe-

"To me the opposite of beauty is not ugliness but complacency."

nomenon. I have spoken (and written) about his "Kafka and His Precursors" on several occasions. When I borrow a composition from another artist's work, or quote a historical painting or conversation in some way, I am excited by the reactivation of the past I feel, as well as the thrill of speaking to the dead, and aligning myself with works of art that move me.

A second important factor concerns limits. I am constantly working to create constraints in my practice—by restricting my materials choice to what is at hand, or by allowing chance processes to determine my color palette—and I find that working with historical references creates another limitation.

Thirdly, and this relates closely to the last point, I am interested in strategies of removing arbitrary decisions in my practice, and the act of quoting an existing artwork is one way to circumvent a degree

106 of invention. Of course, the choice of what to quote is highly subjective. Nevertheless, once that first decision is made, working within the limits it establishes is less demanding in a helpful way, if that makes any sense. I like to set up a formula, and then take it to its logical conclusion by executing it. **DR** I like what you said earlier about honoring, updating, and contradicting. That is a healthy trifecta. As you know, I've begun a

felt the presence of Stevens more than any other voice, and in this one, even though two poems invoke and evoke Neruda, I feel like Rilke is everywhere. I hear him in almost every poem in the book.

The most prominent figure in the book, however, is Paul Klee. There are five poems about or in response to Klee's paintings or aesthetic theory—he gets more real estate than any poet. In fact, when we were talking earlier

> *"I don't think of Klee as a political artist, but I see him using art as a form of resistance."*

new project in which I am writing poems in response to Cy Twombly drawings [see poems in this issue], and I feel like I am doing these three things and about 72 others. In *Self-Portrait*, I enter into conversations with Neruda, Wallace Stevens, Rainer Maria Rilke, Adrienne Rich, and Langston Hughes. Each of these poems honors, updates, and contradicts their greatness. In my first book, I

about painting and emotion, I was thinking about Klee's famous line, "One eye sees, the other feels." I think, too, about how … dangerous … Hitler found Klee's work. In 1937, seventeen of Klee's pieces were included in the infamous Degenerate Art Exhibition and over 100 were seized by the Nazis. I don't think of Klee as a political artist, but I see him using art as a form of resistance—just like

Neruda, just like Stevens, just like Hughes, just like Rich, just like Rilke.

JK Adorno stated once that all totalizing narratives identify with systems of power, which I take to mean oppression. I hope that art can be one way to act against these powers which, under the guise of consensus, make claims to truth, normalcy, identity, etc. The diversity of approaches in my studio practice—in mediums, styles, imagery, etc.—not only reflects the breadth of my interests, but also my conscious refusal of the idea that an artist "should" work in only one way to create reliable and identifiable product. That is the logic of the art market—and of art that is consumed in soundbite form, superficially—and is far from what I hope for, and aspire to. Perhaps this is a long way of saying that I believe a refusal to conform to consistent meanings and forms is political, and indeed contemporary, if not necessarily topical.

DR Indeed. To refuse to conform—to resist totalizing narratives, even "only" in the arts—was a matter of life and death at many moments in history, and crucially remains true for our own. ❧

Jordan Kantor writes on a wide range of contemporary art subjects, and holds a professorship at California College of the Arts, where he teaches artistic practice and theory and currently serves as chair of the Painting/Drawing Program.

Dean Rader co-edited Bullets into Bells: Poets and Citizens Respond to Gun Violence *(Beacon Press), an anthology praised by the* New York Times, Poets & Writers, *the* Washington Post, NPR, *and PBS. Rader also writes about poetry and visual culture for a variety of publications such as the* San Francisco Chronicle, Los Angeles Review of Books, Huffington Post, *and* BOMB. *He is a professor at the University of San Francisco.*

OCTET: A FRAGMENT

DEAN RADER

Cy Twombly, *Untitled (To Sappho)*, 1976

black line

/

blank page

/

did I write *page?* I meant *canvas* [so I wrote *page*]

/

[I am beginning to believe that everything might be about its own making]

/

did I say *write?* I meant *draw* [watch me write *line*]

/

[every word is a mark of its own failure]

/

Did I write *word?* I meant *images,* so I drew *line*

/

[to solve the problem of language,] you need language

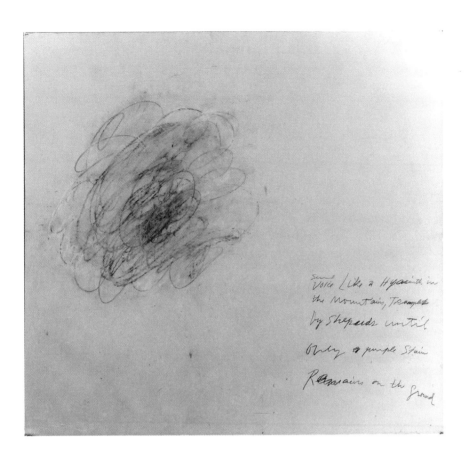

CY TWOMBLY

Untitled (To Sappho), Rome, 1976
© Cy Twombly Foundation; courtesy: Cy Twombly Foundation

UNFINISHED SONNET

DEAN RADER

Cy Twombly, *Untitled* (1971)

I've been thinking about lines of music as furrows in a field.

I've been thinking about paper as a field of pure becoming without being.

I've been thinking about transition—

                             show me where absence stops.

I used to know what the pencil wanted.

I felt I knew what the hand needed from the pencil.

I felt I thought the way birds know air—

                             everything is transference:

CY TWOMBLY

Untitled, Rome, 1971
© Cy Twombly Foundation; courtesy: Cy Twombly Foundation
photo: Belisario Manicone, Rome

PHOTOGRAPHY, STORYTELLING, AND THE INHOSPITABLE WORLD

HEATHER ALTFELD

"It is just possible that photography is the prophecy of a human memory yet to be socially and politically achieved."

—John Berger

In the late 1930s, the photographer Roman Vishniac was dispatched by the Joint Jewish Distribution Committee to take photographs in Eastern Europe for the purposes of international fundraising. Or, according to a different version of the story Vishniac liked to tell, he had been sent "on an assignment from God" to document the plight of rural Jews. Both stories, perhaps, are true. One of the photographs that has stayed with me most shows an orderly line of young Jewish children from an elementary school waiting on a dusty road somewhere in Carpathian Ruthenia to take a mikveh, or ritual bath. The children face away from the camera, excepting one, who looks straight at us in his neat waistcoat and black hat. There is a half-dimple visible on his right cheek.

Looking at the children assembled in such a line is unsettling. If I had not known, from the caption, that these were elementary students waiting for a *mikveh*, I might have thought this to be a picture of one **113** of the earliest deportations. There is a certain irony in the fact that they are waiting to bathe. The past, in this case, seems to evoke the future, rather than the other way around. So the photograph's caption offers a kind of relief—this isn't a death march, it is a dusty country road several years before the war. However, that relief lasts only until one remembers that of the roughly 100,000 Jews in this region, only about 10,000 to 12,000 survived the deportations and death camps. Few if any of these children likely lived much longer.

Vishniac took more than 16,000 photographs of Jewish citizens during the late 1930s. Many of them lived in remote rural regions in what is now Eastern Slovakia and Western Ukraine. Some of the negatives were smuggled out of Europe before and during the war; some may never be found. Vishniac's daughter, Mara Vishniac Kohn, recently gifted much of his extant collection to The Magnes Collection of Art and Jewish Life. Vishniac attempted on a number of occasions to elicit the attention of the American government, sending five photographs with a letter to FDR for his birthday. "I fled, and everywhere I was a stranger...And then came Hitler, and I saw the most horrible that our generation and generations before us ever witnessed. I saw infinite disaster and injustice, and I took it in as sadness and disappointment in Providence." He invited Eleanor Roosevelt to his exhibition at Teacher's College, Columbia University, in 1943, though she did not attend. He did receive the following thoughtful response from Joseph W. Haden, Coordinator of Information at the United States Office of Strategic Services:

"May we assure you of our appreciation for your kindness and the trouble to which you were put to make these excellent photographs available to us.

"They will be very valuable in the work this Division is carrying on."

The note from Haden was dated July 2, 1942. It was the same day that 81 children, the only Jews who remained from the Lidice Massacre of 340 people in Czechoslovakia, arrived at the extermination camp at Chelmno, where they were murdered in Magirus gas vans.

Thinking about Vishniac's photographs—an incredible selection of them can be found on the International Center of Photography's website—has brought me back into conversation with the work of John Berger. I discovered Berger while studying Medical Anthropology at Columbia University through his book *A Fortunate Man*, a collaboration with photographer Jean Mohr, which is a photo essay about the life of Dr. John Eskell, the "fortunate man" of the title. Eskell, or "Sassall," as Berger refers to him, was a physician in the rural U.K. For months, he allowed his life and surroundings to serve as the object of Mohr's camera and of Berger's micro-ethnographic inquiries. The resulting book is, among other things, a study of a profession that, not unlike the Jewry of Europe, has all but disappeared. This was the "ministry" of medicine, the sort of personal, attentive, deeply felt healing that had been practiced by physicians for centuries; a world in which physicians made house calls, delivered babies, diagnosed and treated illness, depression, set bones, stitched cuts. Sassall was there at their births and through the trials of their lives, and in many cases, was present for their deaths. He knew the intimate details of their lives, but because of his role in the community, guarded them as private. The book is an evocation of medicine as a tender practice in another era. Sterilized by the medicine of the present, it is also in part a museum piece. This is what it looked like, once upon a time, to be a doctor.

Berger often sounds in his writing like an oracle, or a hierophant, or a prophet. He worked to see, and to reveal, hidden truths in art, in photography, in images. The hidden depths of culture and politics and daily life. The inextricable ties between capitalism and suffering.

He thought, and wrote constantly, obsessively, about loss—lost ways **115**
of life, lost ways of thinking, a sense of loss, as he himself said in an
interview with Michael Silverblatt, "that is directed toward the future."
The nature of storytelling via photography and narrative was Berger's
lifelong concern. "Storytelling," he said in an interview with Philip
Maughan, "does not begin with inventing, it begins with listening." He
spent a lot of his life listening—listening to the peasants of the village
he chose to live in, to migrant workers, to photographs. His various
projects, which included novels, plays, poetry, interviews, monographs,
literary essays, and two other photographic collaborations with Jean
Mohr—A Seventh Man and Another Way of Telling—tell the story of a
storyteller. Berger is most well-known, perhaps, for his prescient book
and subsequent television series Ways of Seeing.

Decades ago, in his essay "Uses of Photography," which in large part
was written as a response to the work collected in Susan Sontag's 1977
book, On Photography, Berger was already calling for an "alternative
photography" which would incorporate photography into social and
political memory, "instead of using it as a substitute which encourages
the atrophy of any such memory." It is in this essay that he makes
a distinction between being a recorder and a reporter, a distinction
marked by the way that images are "addressed to those suffering what
they depict." This distinction, he says, is crucial.

"The secret of true storytelling," Berger said in 2015, in one of
his last interviews, "is to try to establish a relationship of hospitality
towards the listener or reader. Storytelling is a collaboration not only
between the storyteller and what he is telling, and the people he is talking
about, but, first and foremost, with the reader. And this question of
hospitality. Of trying to come to an understanding." Cryptic, yes. But
it is something I have been chewing on, this relationship between the
storyteller and hospitality. Berger credited a good deal of his thinking

116 about storytelling to Walter Benjamin, whose essay "The Storyteller" was an immense influence. "The art of storytelling," Benjamin warned, "is coming to an end... One reason for this phenomenon is obvious: experience has fallen in value."

Many anthropologists think about hospitality as an essential element of human culture, a way to forge relationships with outsiders and strangers. In A.M. Hocart's 1927 essay "The Divinity of the Guest," he asserts that in numerous world cultures, "Not only is the god present with the stranger, but the stranger is often a god." Hospitality forms the basis for many of our rituals. It contains an implicit sense of reciprocation, and in this reciprocation there is a kind of equality formed. It requires one to "lay aside the spear" as anthropologist Marcel Mauss wrote, or as Nietzsche put it, causes a "paralysis" of "enmity in the stranger."

The rich exchanges between storytelling and empathy are essential tasks for us, as writers and artists and photographers. This was what Berger had hoped *A Fortunate Man* would do—that it would be read and seen by future generations who were trying to understand ways of creating solidarity and community in an era where we are increasingly distanced from one another.

Much of Berger's work concerned the plight of migrant workers and refugees. His book *A Seventh Man,* written in 1973–1974, depicts fragments from the lives of migrant workers in Europe. In the introduction, he tells us plainly and without apology that these are European male migrant workers and that the book does not tell the stories of immigrants from former colonial territories, or women. The former set of stories, he tells us, "belong to the history of colonialism and neo-colonialism." As for women, he notes that he hopes their stories will be told, too, but that this would have to constitute a separate project. "This century," Berger writes, "is the century of emigration, enforced and voluntary. That is to say, a century of partings without end, and a century haunted by the memories of those partings." **117**

A *Seventh Man* is an encapsulation of Berger's preoccupation with the forced global movement of humans from rural to urban areas due to the entrapments of capitalism. But because, as he writes in the introduction to *Ways of Seeing*, "Seeing comes before words," this is a book that relies on the pairing of images to stories. It avoids the trap of depicting the lives of migrant workers through the mechanics of information, the reduction of their experiences to statistical data. This is another clear example of the influence of Walter Benjamin's discussion on the importance of storytelling:

"We recognize that with the full control of the middle class, which has the press as one of its most important instruments in fully developed capitalism, there emerges a form of communication which, no matter how far back its origin may lie, never before influenced the epic form in a decisive way. But now it does exert such an influence ... This new form of communication is information."

Information, Benjamin goes on to say, lays claim to "prompt verifiability." Our senses give us "information," of course, but it is information that is mediated by consciousness. And information, poet Dean Young aptly tells us in his book *The Art of Recklessness*, "is a corpse."

In September 2015, the media brought us images of Aylan Kurdi, a Syrian child drowned and deposited on a beach in Turkey. Many of us saw the photographs of him, his Velcro sneakers still on his feet, one ear upturned to the sky, one ear buried in the sand. One of the reports talked about his long eyelashes. For weeks Aylan's photograph lived inside me. It was, as Berger would perhaps say, one of the "public" uses of photography—the seized appearances that offer information to we who are distant in so many other ways from that lived experience. Except, of course, in this case it was not a lived experience; it was a post-mortem one. Photographs, in a certain way, are always "dead."

118   While they move us, they do not move. They are separated from their subjects the moment they are taken, frozen in the time and place and expression of what Cartier-Bresson referred to as the "decisive moment."

This single photograph prompted a flood of donations to international aid agencies and heightened public awareness of the gravity of the situation in Syria. Researchers working on empathy and humanitarian decision-making wanted to understand the longer-term impact of the photograph of Aylan on the public, so they analyzed data of contributions to aid agencies after the appearance of the photograph in international media in the weeks and months to follow. They also did statistical analysis of Google search terms "Syria," "Refugees," and "Aylan." "This newly created empathy," the same researchers tell us, "waned rather quickly." The image stayed with us long enough to elicit donations to the International Red Cross, and was "worth more than hundreds of thousands of statistical lives," but it did not appear to have enormous long-term fiscal or political impacts.

When NPR covered the analysis of the study, Dr. Paul Slovic, one of the principal researchers, said that he thought one of the reasons the photo had been so widely distributed and had been viewed by so many more people than similar others was that "the child is very young, nicely dressed and looks like he could have been one of our own kids."

Today, 68.5 million refugees roam the planet. Almost 30 million of them are children, who, let's face it, could be our own. Forty-four thousand people a day are forced to flee their homes due to conflict or persecution. But these statistics will not compel us. The image will compel us, perhaps, for a little while. Once the image has faded, what will compel us?

I co-teach a course entitled "Beauty" each fall to Honors students at California State University, Chico. On the first day of class, the first time I taught the course, we met in one of the oldest classrooms on campus—the kind of room that is so dusty and forgotten that it had cubbies for student work, a cloakroom, an old upright piano, the smell of acrylic paints in jars. I asked the students to talk about their experiences of beauty. They talked about untouchable popular girls in high school. Celebrities. "The Media," which brought many nods and a crop of fresh hands in the air. "The media," I say, nodding. "Ahh. Yes. But a distraction from the sort of beauty we want you to think about. What else have you got?" Someone delivered a baby during his summer job as an EMT in training. He said that it was terrifying, but also beautiful. I filed this away; soon enough, we would be reading Rilke's "The First Elegy," in which he writes:

"For beauty is nothing but the beginning of terror, which we are still just able to endure, and we are so awed because it serenely disdains to annihilate us."

One tells about the death of her grandmother. "Her eyes rolled back into her head, so that all you could see were the whites of them. And then they started to bleed, from the corners—my bubbie's eyes had always been so, so blue, but now we were by her bed and seeing the whole other side of them. It was like when you climb to the top of a mountain and you see these other mountains you couldn't see before. It doesn't sound like it, but watching her die was completely beautiful."

It was pretty quiet until a young man raised his hand and said *a massacre. Massacres are beautiful.* Was he fucking with me? First day of class, first female college professor, a room flash-frozen in the year 1979. Usually a quip comes to me, a little poke, part humor, part challenge—*I won't fuck with you, if you don't fuck with me. Deal?* The class waited to see what I would say. I waited to see what I would say. I was waiting for a message to arrive from a distant battlefield, a trench, elsewhere on the planet. A place, perhaps, where unbearable suffering was occurring at this precise moment. He started to describe war. The

120   bent and broken limbs, blood from the open cavity of a chest where the organs, now visible, attempt to reconstruct the body's functions, the sound of a river where men wash their wounds. And for one single strange second, I could see what he saw in this unbearable suite of pain. The well-composed photograph that makes us terrible animals beautiful. The excitement of blood, what Francois Truffaut meant when he said, "There's no such thing as an anti-war film." But this boy does not have the story of the pain. The agony has been etherized upon contact with what Berger calls "the violence of the fission" between their pain and this moment. So agony does not arrive here in Chico, California, at half past four on a Wednesday. Nothing happens. We move on. Class dismissed.

Given the limitations of photographic images, and even computer-generated images, one can imagine a more immersive simulation of war for the American public. A full-sensory simulation, delivered to us with a click on one of our handy devices. Like Mike Teevee of Roald Dahl's *Charlie and the Chocolate Factory*, this would reduce to invisible particulate the elemental scents and tastes and skin sensations of actually "being there" in the comfort of your own home. The Scentee Machina, an iPhone dongle that plugs into the headphone jack, can be programmed to release a burst of rose, lavender, or buttered-potato scent to accompany text messages and alarms. There is the experimental Bluetooth-enabled device, the Cyrano Scent Machine, which can transmit up to twelve aromas (currently largely marketed for car-freshening purposes, but surely these limits are temporary). Dr. Nimesha Ranasinghe, an engineer at the National University of Singapore, is on the cutting edge of devising electrical and thermal stimulation to stimulate the tip of the human tongue *non-invasively* in order to produce primary taste sensations such as salty, sour, sweet, bitter. "In a gaming environment we could come up with a new reward system based on taste sensations. For example, if you complete a game task successfully or complete a level, we can

give a sweet, minty or sour reward. If you fail, we can deliver a bitter   **121**
message." Soon the sounds and visions, the thud of bodies, or parts of
bodies, hitting the ground, the Wonka-esque ability to smell the pits
of open sewage, the raw ripped skin, the smoke of the crematorium,
will be an app. Depending on the audience, corporations could market
it as a realistic, action-packed feast for the senses, or, when visiting
educational institutions, as an "empathetiscope"—for what could make
our children and young people more compassionate than actual sensory
footage of carnage?

Children live almost fully in the sensory world. This seems self-
evident to anyone who has ever spent five minutes around a child,
but because we don't necessarily believe it unless it is proven to us,
there are aisles and aisles of books on parenting based on decades
of research that cite the importance of imaginative play, of limiting
screen time, maximizing outdoor time and tactile experiences, and so
forth. Nevertheless, we persist in endangering childhood by limiting
the imaginative life that accompanies sensory experience. Boredom is
anathema to today's modern child, but more probably, to today's modern
parent. Walter Benjamin calls boredom "the apogee of mental relaxation…
Boredom is the dream bird that hatches the egg of experience."

The child's separation from the sensory universe is another sort of
violent fissure. The indoor child, spending much of their days sitting
still at a desk, with a screen, trained for entertainment at an appallingly
early age, is severed from the sensory connections essential to empathy.
Sensations of pain, comfort, discomfort, fear, joy, love, nurturing arise
in part from contact with the living world. If the environment is an
abstraction, a distant landscape, something that exists outside a window
or a screen, it is hard to fully feel its pain. The war is inside the screen,
not alongside me. The image—photographic or computer-generated—
requires us to have a certain kind of metaphoric context. We see beads

of sweat on someone's forehead and know that when the photograph was taken, they were hot. We see blood, and imagine their pain. To be understood, to be meaningful, the photograph requires some sense of its story and a relationship to the tangible world.

I printed a copy of Susan Sontag's 2002 article from *The New Yorker*, "Looking at War: Photography's View of Devastation and Death," for my student, the one who believed in the beauty of the massacre. In this essay, she writes, "The photograph is like a quotation, or a maxim or a proverb.... [Photographs] were a record of the real—incontrovertible, as no verbal account, however impartial, could be... since a machine was doing the recording. And they bore witness to the real, since a person had been there to take them." She goes on to note that "Each of us mentally stocks hundreds of photographs, subject to instant recall... The hunt for more dramatic (as they're often described) images drives the photographic enterprise, and is part of the normality of a culture in which shock has become a leading stimulus of consumption and source of value." For the student, I underline the passage where she writes, "The understanding of war among people who have not experienced war is now chiefly a product of the impact of these images."

He reads it, willingly, and comes to my office hour a week later. "I didn't understand all of it," he says. "But I looked at a lot of the photographs she mentions. I mean, I see what she is saying. War isn't always a great thing. But I still think massacres can be beautiful."

Two years into its run, in June 1859, *The Atlantic Monthly* printed an essay by Oliver Wendell Holmes, who would go on, of course, to become the oldest Chief Justice of the Supreme Court. The essay, "The Stereoscope and the Stereograph," was a commentary on the possibilities of photography. "This triumph of human ingenuity," he writes, "is the most audacious, remote, improbable, incredible—the one that would seem least likely to be regained, if all traces of it were lost, of all the **123** discoveries man has made.... Form is henceforth divorced from matter. In fact, matter as a visible object is of no great use any longer, except as the mould on which form is shaped. Give us a few negatives of a thing worth seeing, taken from different points of view, and that is all we want of it. Pull it down or burn it up, if you please.... We have got the fruit of creation now, and need not trouble ourselves with the core. Every conceivable object of Nature and Art will soon scale off its surface for us."

This was during the days of silver-coated copper plates, and the exposure time of film was long—not quite so much like the "violent fissure" Berger talks about. Thus, Holmes is being somewhat speculative when he writes that, "The next European war will send us stereographs of battles. It is asserted that a bursting shell can be photographed. The time is perhaps at hand when a flash of light, as sudden and brief as that of the lightning which shows a whirling wheel standing stock still, shall preserve the very instant of the shock of contact of the mighty armies that are even now gathering. The lightning from heaven does actually photograph natural objects on the bodies of those it has just blasted—so we are told by many witnesses."

Among others who have written about photography, Berger tells us that photography is a language, and that this language may very well be one of our strongest forms of perception. Depth psychologist Robert Romanyshyn talks about this form of perception, and perspective, as a "despotic eye." In his essay by the same title, he contemplates the significance of linear perspective in our inventions, and in our "vision"—the eye, in its supremacy, creates a kind of "ocularcentrism of modernity" that tempers the importance of our other senses. It is through this limited vision that we become spectators rather than participants. Considering the photographic image—its limits, and its

124 preoccupations—I wonder if, like super-tasters, there are super-seers, those among us who can look at a photograph of Aylan Kurdi, or any other dying child, and "see" more deeply than the rest of us. And that we could even cultivate this sort of seeing, so that it heightens our empathies rather than diluting them. Photography on steroids, so to speak. One of the thrilling possible features of the *empathetiscope*.

Photographer Sebastião Salgado spent ten years photographing refugees for one of his long-term projects, *Migrations,* chronicling the movement of people due largely to political and environmental circumstances. I first saw his pictures in Wim Wenders's compelling documentary about Salgado's life and work, *The Salt of the Earth*. At one point, Salgado tells us, "We humans are terrible animals. Our history is a history of wars. It's an endless story, a tale of madness. You felt that the whole planet was covered in refugee tents... I lost faith in our species. I didn't believe it was possible for us to live any longer. I had never imagined that man could be part of a species capable of such cruelty to its own members and I couldn't accept it."

Salgado does not simply want to make us feel when we look at his photos. "If the person looking at these pictures only feels compassion, I will believe that I have failed completely," Salgado tells John Berger. "I want people to understand that we can have a solution. Very few of the persons photographed are responsible for the situation that they are now in. Many of them don't understand why they are on the road with thousands of others.... They are not the reason for their being there." Berger himself notes that most photographs are of suffering, and most of that suffering is man-made.

Nevertheless, Salgado has been criticized by many—including Susan Sontag and Ingrid Sischy, former art critic for *The New Yorker*—for making photographs that are "too beautiful." Sischy thought that Salgado was controlling our viewing through an "art direction" that "runs on a kind of emotional blackmail" and is in large part successful at doing so because of our sympathy and guilt. Sichy may be overestimating us. We do not seem prone to being blackmailed these days. Salgado took many photos of migrant children, which call to mind photographs circulating in recent media of the thousands of children caged on United States soil as a result of inhumane separation policies. These photos—beautifully shot or no—invoke an almost mythic lack of American hospitality. Maggie Nelson writes of the Internet's "smorgasboard of human suffering" which has "an eerily leveling effect on the content and context.... Do I or don't I want to watch a Tibetan pilgrim being shot dead by the Chinese police...How about cell phone footage of a man being hung upside-down and sodomized with a rod in an Egyptian prison?" The ease by which these images come to us and leave us disconnects us from any question of empathy, beautiful or no. Is it the image, then, that has failed?

By the end of the year, my student has taken two classes with me. The second, a companion to the first, is called "Virtue." In this class, we read all of Arendt's *Eichmann in Jerusalem* and selections from *The Origins of Totalitarianism*. We show *Night and Fog*, the 1955 French Holocaust film, filmed in the camps before they were sanitized and scrubbed of blood and urine and feces and the acrid lingering smell of death. We read Stephen Mitchell's translation of the Book of Job. We read Wallace Shawn's *Aunt Dan and Lemon*. We talk about empathy, about altruism, about radical evil. Just before summer break, he tells me that he wants to transfer to West Point in the fall. Could I write him a letter?

I can't, I say. I'm so sorry. If you want a letter to go somewhere else, anywhere else, I will write you one. But I can't.

Because you're a liberal and don't believe in war?

I feel like a child who has been caught doing something they were

126 not quite supposed to, and has to decide between sheer honesty and one of those ballooning lies used to extract yourself from punishment.

I am afraid of pain, I say. *All pain. Even other people's pain. I cannot recommend you so that you will eventually and inevitably attend a war. Or to kill anyone, maim, or even send orders to do so. It would be as though I were directly connected to someone's suffering.*

I have no righteous feelings about this. I do not think it was an act of, as John Berger would say, "hospitality." Maybe it was even selfish; I do not want his, or anyone else's, blood on my hands. When he did not get into West Point, I was elated. Perhaps he will find something else to do with his life, I thought to myself. Perhaps this is one of those moments where there is an opening for something different. Instead, he enlists.

What is true: other photographers had documented Eastern European Jews around the same time, for many reasons—genealogical reasons, notions of the exotic. But after Vishniac? After Vishniac, the photographs of the Jews of Europe are primarily of the death-camps and beyond. Sontag writes that her life was basically divided into two. There was her life before she saw the photographs of Dachau, and there was her life after.

Upon the release in 1947 of *Polish Jews,* the first volume of Vishniac's photography published in the United States, and as part of a larger excoriation of the slim volume, critic Harold Rosenberg wrote, "The fault of this book lies in the mistaken idea of whoever is responsible for the selection, that Jews should be pictured as pure spirit, stuck in stores, tenements, and synagogues—in brief, as only accidentally human. I do not find that this commonplace idealism is made more valid by the fact that the 500-year-old mother group of Judaism has been tragically destroyed. Too artistic and too spiritual, *Polish Jews* has in it something of the false funeral oration that conceals the true beauties of the dead by detaching them from the body that was once alive."

I find myself thinking about the student often, especially every 127 fall, when I teach the Rilke elegy. *Beauty is nothing but the beginning of terror.* After years of reading this line, I still do not know what it means. But this year just before teaching the poem, I rewatched Ari Folman's film *Waltz with Bashir* and wish that I had shown it to my student. It is in part a political testimony of the role the Israel Defence Forces played in the 1982 massacre of Lebanese citizens committed by Christian Phalangists in the Shatila and Sabra refugee camps. It is also an exploration of the capacity and limits of human memory and the human ability to alter or repress the most traumatic events. Because it is animated, the audience to a certain degree experiences a double disassociation from atrocity—the layers of screen and manufactured images dilute the reality. The main character is a middle-age Israeli man who is trying to recover his memories of his role in the war with Lebanon. At one point he speaks with an expert in PTSD about the fog in which he has lived all these years. She tells him that one of her clients who was in Beirut during the siege told himself to think of it as a long day trip. "I told myself, what great scenes! Shooting, artillery, wounded people, screaming..." He had looked at everything as through an "imaginary" camera. But then, his "camera" broke when he entered the Beirut Hippodrome and saw the field full of slaughtered Arabian horses. The mechanism that had allowed him to disassociate from the agony was gone.

The mechanism inside of us breaks, too, in the last seven minutes of the film. The animation stops and we see actual footage of the massacre. The images of bloated bodies in the rubble and the cries of women in the streets. Our fog dissipates. There is nothing beautiful to see here. Only horror, terror.

I wonder if the student has been broken of this idea of beauty. I would like to ask him, but he is long gone. Last I heard, he was at a base

128 somewhere in the South, preparing to depart for Afghanistan, where he can shoot his own footage of whatever terrors he finds to be beautiful.

John Sassall committed suicide fifteen years after the publication of *A Fortunate Man*. My memories of him—a man I never knew!—were constructed entirely through Mohr's photographs and Berger's accompanying essay, and when I found out about his death, these memories became part of a strange nostalgia. A kind of *saudade* for a medicine I never knew. A nostalgia for a lost way of life. A nostalgia for his life. A realization and a reconciliation that the idealized sort of medicine he practiced wasn't so ideal—that perhaps it was a form of hospitality so consuming that it swallowed him. One of the most beautiful photographs in the book is a pensive close-up of him smoking a cigarette. In light of his suicide, revisiting the photo, separated from the story of his life and his death, he could be either doctor or patient.

Berger said little about Sassall's death, but in an afterword to the 1999 edition of the book, he writes:

"John the man I loved killed himself. And yes, his death has changed the story of his life. It has made it more mysterious. Not darker … I do not search for what I might have foreseen and didn't—as if the essential was missing from what passed between us; rather I now begin with his violent death, and, from it, look back with an increased tenderness on what he set out to do and what he offered to others, for as long as he could endure."

We are, for a while, invited into Sassall's life—where his solicitousness remains frozen in the time and place constructed for us by this book. All of Berger's writings, in fact, are repeated invitations to look deeply into the world. In *Ways of Seeing*, he whispers the words of Robert Capa right to us as though we were next to him. "If your pictures aren't good enough, you're not close enough."

The Salgados and the Arbuses, the Folmans and the Vishniacs, all make valiant attempts—whether too beautiful or too real—to show us that our human empathy too often fails us. Through the worlds inside **129** of worlds inside of lenses and screens, we watch, or we don't, those who survive, and those who do not, in the endless rotation of earthquakes, hurricanes, fire, flood, war. The faces of strangers circulate past us and through us as though their suffering was an inextricable element in the laws of planetary motion. Click now, to donate, or do not click at all.

Get closer, John is telling us. *Get closer.* ❧

Heather Altfeld is a recipient of the Robert H. Winner Award from the Poetry Society of America. Her poems have appeared in Narrative Magazine, Pleiades, *and* Poetry Northwest *and most recently in* Issue No. 114.

SEEING THINGS

JOHN FREEMAN

Now the trees rush, crackle
in the dark. I sleep like a
sailor on night watch. I was told,
look in the shadows for figures
that
      freeze. Cold has made
it easy. I can see straight
through the park. There
are the camps. There beds.
There, a man, washing his foot
in rain water. You do not
need to be a hawk to
see any of this. No one talks
of this, how winter—
by removing—doesn't just
strip bare, it allows us to see
what's always been there.

STITCH

JOHN FREEMAN

They wore white breasts, like scarves, their hundred heads turned to
us from the blue wood, making the eyes seem like parts of one large
invisible body only gradually showing itself in stripes of winter, she
talking as they strode ahead in car coats and wellingtons, striding
across the grounds talking of how she allowed him to pay and
then paid his bills, he likes to feel, like a man, the two of us behind,
talking of her, as usual, while I wanted to say, don't you see that
hillside that moving hillside right there? But it was backdrop, part
of the perpetual park in which they lived, part of the design, here is
nature, here are some new guests, the game recast, before new eyes
or ears, in this season or that and the eyes, they watched in hundreds,
wanting to know, were we good, did we mean well, and on that day I
could not speak my answer.

. . . .

John Freeman is the author of Maps *(Copper Canyon Press) and teaches writing at The New School.*
His interview with Arundhati Roy appeared in Issue No. 113.

PACIFIC

PETER ORNER

After Andre Dubus's "At Night"

She sat calm and motionless in the living room while they worked on her husband upstairs. There's something so assuring about these people who tromp into your house out of the night. She'd always been a socialist and saw these men, and this one woman who's in charge, with their dark blue uniforms and heavy boxes and unperturbable faces, as physical proof of the ultimate (potential) goodness of government. It wasn't the first time they'd come. Nor was it the second. If he made it through this time, she was under no illusions that a night wasn't coming soon when he wouldn't.

She sat in the living room amid their work. He was a sculptor; she was a potter. When people asked what the difference was since they both worked with clay, she'd say, "The stuff I make is useful." And this was true. She made bowls. He made heads. Both of them always had day jobs. She'd been a librarian; he, an accountant.

The day jobs were a front.

On weekends, when they were younger, they'd attend craft fairs all over Northern California. Sonoma, Napa, Solano, Contra Costa, San Joaquin. A few times they'd driven up to Humboldt. Once all the way to Oregon. They'd set up a card table and a couple of umbrellas. What better way to see places we wouldn't normally see! That's what she always told the children as they repacked all their unsold pieces **133** back into the trunk of the car.

She'd have to call them in the morning and tell them. Maybe not tomorrow morning, but soon. She sat in the living room, hardly listening to the commotion in the bedroom. She'd heard it all before. What fuss over a failing body, as if it wasn't designed to ultimately fall completely apart. She gazed at their work in the half dark. The work of their hands. The rest of the world, she knew damn well, including their kids, thought them both a little bonkers. This room, the bedrooms, the kitchen, the bathroom, the front stoop. There was never enough room for their work. New pieces crowded out old pieces, heads and bowls, heads and bowls. After they retired, it was as though they'd been spurred on by a kind of delirious compulsion. Not to stave off anything, but simply because they'd had the stamina to go on working. Let it not make sense.

"Ruby?"

"Yes?"

"Fred's medications, do you happen to—"

She recited them one by one by one, a litany, a chant.

The past few years they'd begun to shrink. In town, people said they'd become almost identical. This is often said of elderly people, but even she had to admit that in their case it was almost uncanny. They'd become dead ringers for each other. Same height, same wobbly gait. Really, from a distance, you couldn't tell one from the other.

The dog died. The other dog died. Still, every day they walked across the sewer ponds and then to the ocean. You could stand there two hours, you could stand there five minutes. The Pacific didn't give a hoot about time. It would eat a year for breakfast. Is that why they'd always been so drawn to it? Is that why, still, they came and stood at the edge, day after day? Its blessed indifference? ❧

NAKED MAN HIDES

PETER ORNER

Everybody knows this. Sometimes you lose everything, including your clothes. I must have taken them off at some point after the crash. I can't remember. I must have felt hot. How else to explain why I took off all my clothes? Helene came to jail the next morning and showed me the paper and we even laughed about it, at first. Above the fold: *Naked Man Hides After Crash*. They'd never given anybody much of a reason to buy the *Independent Journal* before. I should get a cut of the sales. Helene said she hadn't come to bail me out this time. I said, "When have you ever?" That's when she started to cry. She wanted me to understand what I'd become, as if I didn't know it. She thought shoving a headline in my face would help me see in black and white what everybody else saw. Not just our kids, my parents, her parents, my sister, but everybody in San Rafael. You went to college to end up here? I told her if I had any shame left I'd yank it out of my throat and stuff it down again. Helene threw the paper on the floor and stood up and knocked on the little window to let the guard know she wanted out. She stooped, picked up the paper, and left. Maybe she'll paste the article in one of her scrapbooks.

They brought me back to the cell and I sat there and trembled, for hours. It was hell, of course, but it's also a little like having the chills when you've got the flu. You're grateful because that seizing your body's doing helps keep you warm. I'd gone from so hot to so cold. Must have been hours sitting there. I remember at some point they tried to give me lunch. I couldn't look at the food. Same later on with a dinner tray. Before lights out, they brought in two new guys. Because I'd been in there alone, I'd taken the single. These two got the bunk. They each took a long piss and went to bed. At eleven, they turn the lights down, not off completely, and I sat there in what passed for darkness. You know how your eyes adjust to the little light there is. I looked across the cell, which was maybe seven by nine, and saw the two sleepers, both of them wrapped in white sheets up to their necks. The fat one was on the bottom. He was a stranger to me. I'd seen the skinny one around town. I was still shaking but like I say some part of me almost half-enjoyed it. There was a blanket I could have pulled around my shoulders but I didn't. Amazing what our bodies are designed to take. Helene says I'm looking at five to six on a good day, if the judge got laid the night before and had some waffles for breakfast. Eight to ten, at least, if he didn't get much sleep and was suffering from an upset stomach. Possession of a controlled substance, driving under the influence of said controlled substance, driving under the influence of another controlled substance, unlawful taking of a vehicle, reckless driving, fleeing the scene of an accident, failure to follow a lawful order, resisting—

"It was your car, Hennie."

"How was I supposed to get to work? Who was going to pick up the kids? In what?"

But what I'm trying to say is that while I was watching those guys sleep, just two guys snoring, coughing, gurgling, moving around, changing positions, trying to get comfortable on those slack mattresses, I felt something, let's say, beyond my immediate predicament. My mother once took me and my sister Francis to a museum. We were in Chicago visiting cousins. It was an Egyptian museum, what it was doing in

136 Chicago, who knows, but there were these mummies in glass cases and I remember how I pressed my nose against the glass and stared at the wrapped-up body of a woman and wondered what she'd make of me, some ten-year-old—what, almost two thousand years later?—snooping on her infinite sleep. My nostrils up against the glass. You know how it makes you look like a pig? I was doing that. Oink, oink. I wanted to get as close as I possibly could. I whispered hello to her head, to her old head wrapped in that yellowed burlap—was it burlap they used? Hello? Francis asked, Who are you talking to? And I said, Who do you think I'm talking to?

It was like that with these two guys. I was only trying to get close, to establish a little camaraderie across the chasm. Do I make any sense? Except with these two I didn't need to move toward them at all. My two fellow fuckups asleep in white sheets. I didn't need to move an inch. I swear, from my bunk, I stroked their faces without needing my hands. The skinny one had stubble. I felt it grow beneath my fingers. The fat one was clean-shaven, his face slicked with sweat. And I thought, holy fuck, we're not dead. Together, we're not dead. As in not dead yet. Think of all the years we will be. Our bodies turn to caramel. You with the tiny sprouting tendrils of facial hair. You with the sweat-wet cheeks. Together at this moment, I thought—don't laugh at me, Hennie—we are not dead. You think this isn't a net positive? ✄

Peter Orner is the author of two novels, two story collections, and the memoir Am I Alone Here? *(Catapult). His newest story collection,* Maggie Brown & Others, *will be published in July by Little, Brown.*

DIANA GUERRERO-MACIÁ

Yes, 2017, wool, oil paint, bleach, cotton,
Belgian linen on quilt and grommeted canvas, 76 × 56 inches
courtesy: the artist and Traywick Contemporary, Berkeley; photographed by Lara Kastner

DIANA GUERRERO-MACIÁ

The Other Ones no. 6, 2018, oil, acrylic, pigment, India ink on felt, cotton, and linen, 17 × 14 inches
courtesy: the artist and Traywick Contemporary, Berkeley; photographed by Lara Kastner

DIANA GUERRERO-MACIÁ

The Other Ones no. 12, 2018, oil, acrylic, pigment, India ink
on felt, cotton, and linen, 17 × 14 inches
courtesy: the artist and Traywick Contemporary, Berkeley; photographed by Lara Kastner

DIANA GUERRERO-MACIÁ

Now is the Winter, 2018, oil, acrylic, pigment, India ink on felt, cotton, and linen, 17 × 14 inches
courtesy: the artist and Traywick Contemporary, Berkeley; photographed by Lara Kastner

DIANA GUERRERO-MACIÁ

Backside no. 6, 2018, wool, thread, and collage on archival pigment print, 25 × 21 inches
courtesy: the artist and Traywick Contemporary, Berkeley; photographed by Claire Britt

DIANA GUERRERO-MACIÁ

The Tempest, 2008, wool, vinyl, and cotton on canvas, 60 × 60 inches
courtesy: the artist and Traywick Contemporary, Berkeley; photographed by Tom Van Eynde

DIANA GUERRERO-MACIÁ

A 15th c. Starry Night, 2010, hand-sewn wool, cotton, and leather on canvas, 30 × 23 inches
courtesy: the artist and Traywick Contemporary, Berkeley; photographed by Tom Van Eynde

DIANA GUERRERO-MACIÁ

Front no. 7, 2018, wool, thread, and collage on archival pigment print, 25 × 21 inches
courtesy: the artist and Traywick Contemporary, Berkeley; photographed by Claire Britt

I SWORE I WOULD NEVER BE THE SORT OF WOMAN

CATE LYCURGUS

to sleep on a monogrammed set of sheets, own
a minivan with goldfish crammed down in the gear
shaft. To change her name or license plates; park
herself by a finger lake, let it tide over her thirst
for ocean and its rhythms. Not one to leave
in the eighth inning, to stop a book midway through,
for endings she could not take. I swore there would be
no plucking dark moustache hairs not meant to grow,
no owing money, nor ousting mice from the hollow
of our apricot. I intended not to lose the rooms
expanding in my chest. Or hear my daddy's rattle all day—
like a child tasked to keep tambourines still—
and mutter something mean. Always about
losing the quiet or needing to get up and pull fleece
over his hands once more. Swore I would never
dance alone, drink neat or need some touch so bad
to agree, and agree in a truck. That I would love
a married man, but head on home. Knock-out-punch me
cold before I'd fall asleep in flowery sheets, in light
that smells of leotards and high school chemistry.
I can see molecules built together, charges on the binder
paper—the bind is always history, and what I swore
comes back to me as humble as a Hoosier pie: straight
butter, cornstarch, cream. I was common; all I am
was not my plan as the girl I've let down now,

146   would rather renounce—a body turns over
its cells completely, every seven years. Like telephone
whispered ear to ear, she feared herself garbled
in the passing, bit by replaceable bit. I've abandoned
the girl bent to her knees, sick and heaving chunks
of custard pie into the street. Didn't hold back
her egg-drenched hair, see that she was gut-wrenched,
childless, care to touch the sepia that hounded all
her days. Despite crepe myrtles' inclination ever-more
toward radiance—jonquil, gold—I should have seen—
it followed her, against all odds, ignored her direst
vows. Intent has little to do with it. Resplendence flits
to new-fitted skin: sloughed shoulders, forearms, crown.
I walk adorned, astounded that the girl who knew
no phone numbers by heart nor had the heart to call
out forswore her future, so made sure I'd end up
in it.

Cate Lycurgus's work has appeared in many publications, including Gulf Coast, The Iowa Review, Tin House, *and others. She is the interviews editor at* 32 Poems *and is an instructor at San Jose State University.*

BOND TO THE GIFT GIVER

MIN HAN

My wife has fallen in love with a monkey. Orange-faced, gray-chested, with red-brown trimmed thighs, the fool spent too much time in God's wardrobe and landed himself on the critically endangered list. He's the Old World kind, that's her taste: an anatomically correct replica of the Indochinese *gray-shanked douc langur*. But don't let the name impress you. He's nothing but a stinking, flea-bitten ape that never bothered to learn new adaptations. And now at history's final curtain call, his king-of-the-jungle days are gone.

The *douc* in my house faces no biological threat. He lords over his dominion of high chairs, Legos, and charger cords in a state of arrogant bliss. My wife could spend hours stroking his sleek gray coat. She falls asleep with his scrawny ruff pressed to her cheek, clutching his tasseled tail like the Andon cord of some escape valve.

There he is now, on the top shelf, ogling her as she removes her tailored suit jacket. I see his black eyes scan her up and down, from the slender Thai shoulders to the full milkmaid hips she inherited from her Dutch mother.

"The bronze one, in front of Simmons Hall," my wife is saying, oblivious. She hangs her jacket on a wooden hanger. "I'm sure you've seen it." Seen one, you've seen them all. It's the third day of protests at the Uni—*college*, as they call it here—where my wife teaches

148 Communications. Higher education, it turned out, wasn't Baswell Fleck's only weakness. The school's biggest donor was also tossing chips to KKK affiliates. Now the students want his statue gone, but the administration is on the fence. His family is threatening to cut all support if his statue is removed.

My wife sheds her wrinkled blouse, then inches herself out of the bizarre body sock she's recently bought online. It's designed to hide the sweet band of flesh around her waist that's been expanding since Marcus's birth. I despise that body condom. Makes me feel like I'm hugging a seal in an office outfit.

Frankly, I don't see what the fuss is about. Back home, old Fleck would be two meters deep in Jeffrey's Bay with a rope around his waist. But I know better than to interrupt her now. It's Wednesday movie night—her idea—and I've already put Marcus to bed. She's in a mood, and better to let it blow over than coax her out, or I might have to yawn through another Channel 4 documentary about overweight hoarders in the Lake District.

She takes down the anvil of a black binder from the shelf, and I know what's coming. She'll go downstairs to the den with her herbal teas and Erykah Badu playlist, underline dangling modifiers till she falls asleep with the lights on.

"I thought we were watching a show tonight."

She sighs. "Sorry. Midterm grades were due yesterday."

My wife teaches four sections at the community college. Since some punk accused her online of being "arrogant" (she didn't so much mind), a "slow grader" and the brutal "at times rambly," she's become a tad paranoid. The kid was a royal idiot. My wife has won the department teaching award two years in a row, and her Rate My Professor sizzle score is 4.4. Quality, 4.7. *Four point seven!* How can I describe the feeling of total strangers gushing about your life partner on the most publically accessible billboard on the planet? You'd be hard-pressed to **149** find harsher critics than maladjusted twenty-year-olds in Orange County.

My wife reaches up to retrieve her monkey from the shelf. "Very mature," she says, noticing my handiwork. Earlier today, I cinched the monkey's four black paws together with his long tail.

"Well look at that," I say happily. "The idiot's tangled himself up."

She frees him, and when she sits him on top of her binder, I knock him off and boot him across the room. He soars, light as popcorn. His feathery white ruff billows like a dandelion head.

"I get it, you don't want to be here with me," I say. "You'd rather sit on the monkey's face."

"What?"

"Cut the monkey business for the night." I pull her toward me. "Let's you and me get to know each other."

"You and I," she says, dusting off the stinking ape.

Goddamn, woman. I picture stabbing the monkey with kitchen knives. I picture lighting his tail like a fuse and watching him ignite into a torrid blaze. "Come on, don't make me beg. I'm about to go next door and ask Larry for his supplier."

She puts her hand over her forehead as if checking for a fever. "You do that," she says.

"You two have a lot in common," I say." Larry's got his love bots and you've got your monkey."

"That's absurd," she sputters. I try to catch her in a hug, but she squirms out of my grasp. "Leave me alone. Some of us have *work* to do."

I'm at a loss for words. What right does she have to talk about work when who cooks, who cleans, who fixes the showerhead and wipes the boy and looks up documentaries like a goddamn concierge service—what about that is *not* working? But my wife's binder is already tucked under her arm, monkey in hand, and she's halfway to the door.

150   "I'm ringing Larry," I call after her. "Gonna get me a Pamela. Maybe an Octopussy, too."

Her half wave says *good riddance*. Her tight behind and that asshole's smirk taunt me all the way down the corridor.

✻   ✻   ✻

Larry's backyard is lit up tonight: Sharp white, powerful beams like stadium lights. I go to the bedroom window, the one that overlooks the side of his property, and I stick my head out into the mild evening air. I can just make out a striped bikini against biscuit skin, a beach ball, a wig. Another photo shoot with his silicon ladies. Bloody batty Americans.

The trouble isn't Larry so much as Marcus. My boy's soft, permeable four-year-old brains, brains that soak up everything. It will only be a matter of time before he wants to know what business the neighbor has with dolls.

A few months ago, Larry had one of 'em outside on the front lawn. She had a rack like balloon animals crammed up her chest. Marcus asked, "Does Pop-Pop have a doll, too?" We had just returned from a visit to my father-in-law, an hour's drive over the hills.

"Don't be silly," my wife said. "That's Mr. Small's granddaughter's doll. He's just looking after it." Her explanation had landed surprisingly well. One of the girls at day care had recently received a three-foot-tall Barbie for her birthday.

After that encounter, my wife and I fought for weeks about renewing the lease to our condo. She's still convinced Larry is harmless. If a policeman comes around, there is nothing bad we can say about Larry. But Mom always said to watch for the quiet ones. The man is sick. He ought to be committed. Grown men don't play with dolls without screws loose in their heads.

✻   ✻   ✻

BOND TO THE GIFT GIVER

At half past midnight, my wife shuffles back into the room. She's **151** not as quiet as she thinks she is. When she settles under the blankets, I picture her picking briars and ticks off her monkey's back, sniffing his white rump, nestling him into the crook of her arm.

"No monkeys in bed," I grunt. I've told her a dozen times before. I reach over to shove him off like I usually do, but tonight my wife swats my hand away and lies over him, protecting him with her body.

"It's not my fault you don't like to cuddle," she mutters.

I haven't met anyone who likes cuddling as much as Julia. In our courtship, I endured months of terrible sleep to persuade her I could protect her for the rest of her nights.

I give up and scoot over to hold her. "It's me or the monkey," I warn.

But she yawns and curls up away from me. "Let's just get some sleep. I have meditation sit at seven."

I roll over, close my eyes, try to count down from ten. I try not to think about the time when I could hold her attention in my hand and mold it into any old shape. Since we moved to Southern California, since my income has fallen into an unsteady trickle, since I began to write about the best celery shakes in the greater Los Angeles area, I hold a shrinking sliver of real estate in my wife's time. She doesn't relax. She plans. She picks at the meals I make and turns to her color-coded vegetable plate, the proportions divvied out by fist size. She won't drink past ten, won't smoke the occasional joint with me. It's earplugs and eye mask by midnight, Vipassana in the A.M. She *knows* it drives me mad, this American obsession with checklists. She calls it the only way to survive in Orange County.

I look at her silhouette in the dark room. I see the asshole's grubby paws fondling her bare breasts under her nightshirt, and I can't help it, I reach over and yank him from her arms.

"Hey!" she yelps. She flicks her lamp on. "What was that for?"

152   I chuck him across the room, and he crashes with a satisfying *thunk* against the wall. "Aren't you ashamed? You're a grown woman with a monkey fetish."

She crawls out from the covers and retrieves her toy like a puppy dog. "Me? You're jealous of a stuffed animal."

"How am I supposed to react when you spend all night with the monkey between your legs?"

"Something is *wrong* with you," she hisses.

I snatch the ape out of her hands again. It's too easy, like stealing from a child. I sniff the floppy tail and make a face. "I knew it! Smells like *punani*. What have you been doing? Animal rescue! Animal control!"

"You're sick!" she cries. "You've got … got … bestial fantasies!" She lunges, but I'm too fast. I hold him over her head, out of her reach.

"This thing," I say, shaking his limp body, "This thing belongs in *that* yard, with the other doll-fuckers."

And to prove my point, I push up the window and dangle him over Larry's yard.

Her brow furrows, as if unsure whether to call my bluff.

"Enough," she finally says. "Give it back."

"Why should I?" I tease, enjoying the game now.

"You're wicked," my wife says, in the same tone she reserves for Marcus. She launches toward me in full attack, but then the doorknob turns—we both hear it—and she freezes, spins around.

In the doorway, thumb in his mouth, stands one dear, sleepy-eyed boy. My Marcus.

He studies us for a moment.

"What are you guys doing?"

My wife glowers at me. On her face, anguish mixes with hapless distress. There's no amusement in her scowl. It dawns on me that through all these months of teasing and banter, I didn't actually think she had *feelings* for the ape.

The barest breeze tickles my arm. I'm still holding the monkey over Larry's yard. My son and wife's eyes weigh down on me. How did I end up here, and where along this long chain of events did the path deviate into this foreign territory? I can only see more rows, more monkey games, years of therapy for Marcus. I see it all. And I let go.

✿ ✿ ✿

I met a woman in Luang Prabang, six years ago. She came to me like a feral cat, wary but hungry in a tight yellow dress. We stayed up three nights in Vang Vieng for Lao New Year. We crawled through caves like blind moles and danced until our legs gave way, then floated down rivers on old tires, suds of Beerlao washing our hands. My nose bled. My left eye watered when I laughed. I lost my sunglasses thirty times. In Vientiane, we slept for a week because what else was there to do, then scrubbed each other raw and pink, and dragged ourselves to her parents' friends' vacation homes to stuff ourselves with imported Swiss chocolates. When I smashed mosquitos in our net, she called me her hero. She recited her grandfather's Thai poetry and fell asleep on my chest, her needy legs locking me down like twisted vines.

The woman had a loud voice, but I learned that she was fragile. It was hard to know where she bruised. I had many names for her: Maharani, damsel, my girl.

My girl.

My girl, she sweeps her crying child into her arms. "What are you doing up so late, bub?" she says. She kisses him, soothes him; carries him out of the bedroom. With her free hand she reaches back and shuts the door. Not slam, which would be childish. Not gently, which would be the humane thing to do. The silence rings louder than Marcus's confused sobs.

✼ ✼ ✼

I run a hand over my face. The walls in this condo are probably thinner than the house I grew up in. Pops used to punch holes into the wall when he got angry. That happened a lot. When Arsenal lost, when he was drunk or bored, or when he was mad at one of us for looking at him too long or putting one sugar cube in his tea instead of two. *I'm the boss*, he reminded us all the time.

I punch pillows and hurl them into the wall. It helps a little.

Larry's house is dark now. I shine a light out the window onto the ground and see the curl of a white tail in the shrubs. The insane idea of harpooning the animal with a knife and broomstick thankfully passes. I fling myself onto the bed. Let the monkey rot out there. Serves him right.

But I can't drift off. My body has come to rely on my wife to give my sleep shape. I put on music, something soft: *Astral Weeks*, but Morrison's voice is too whiny. The E string *tremolo* hurts my ears, so I change the decade to 2008. The ragged Belfast Cowboy blunders around the Hollywood Bowl, rambling, "Gotta stop breaking down," like a character in one of Marcus's train cartoons. I loop the track and lie back. I imagine Larry returning from his sunrise walk and spotting the tail in his butterfly bush. I picture my wife after yoga, knocking on his door. The thought bothers me. I'll get the monkey in the morning. By then, God willing, this ice block lodged in my chest will have dissolved.

✼ ✼ ✼

Sometime around six, my wife comes in to rummage for clothes. I listen for the grumble of the engine, the muted creak of the tires edging down the driveway, and when all is quiet again, I check the window. The monkey is still there.

A small morning consolation: I don't know what she told Marcus about last night, but Marcus has no questions for me. He takes his

time at the sink, splashing water, spraying toothpaste foam onto the 155
mirror and basin. I don't mind. That's what men do. They make a mess.
"Say 'mae-ss,'" I tell him. "*Mae-ss.*" He should sound at least a
little like me, even if I don't have much of an accent anymore.

By the time he's finished cereal, he's given himself a bloody paper cut,
asked for a rabbit, a fish, a dinosaur costume, and a trip to Disneyland.

"Wouldn't you rather have a dog?" I ask. I show him a Komodo
dragon on my phone, fish out a plaster for his cut, bookmark a Universal
Studios trip for summer.

Outside, Larry is watering his flowers. They must eat straight
fertilizer, because the daisies are always in bloom. "Howzit, neighbor,"
he chirps. Then enunciating carefully—"Throw down some boerewors
on the braai, chommie?"

Must have practiced that mishmash all morning. I grunt without
turning my head so I don't have to see how happy he is with himself.
The monkey can wait. I strap Marcus into his booster seat, and barrel
down the deserted road.

Another anodyne "SoCal" day. Birds chirrup and rap music sparks
out of convertibles like fizzy pop. A row of plastic palm trees has recently
appeared on one traffic island. Fairy lights are strung up their trunks
to distract from their oddly uniform leaves.

"Let's take the long way round, shall we?" I say, as if Marcus can
do anything about it.

Day care is only a ten-minute drive, but I want to be with my boy.
I want to use my dad prerogative in this enclosed space, keep the world
out of our metal bunker. Because certain types of education end at a
young age, and I have his mind to mold. How Marcus wailed at his
paper cut! If his Pop-Pop saw, I'd have a red backside.

My father's view of manhood: A man provides for his children,
his wife, his mother. He speaks little, can take a joke and jab; fixes the

156 house and draws his wallet the way a soldier can be expected to draw his sword—on command; a man is feared but always fair, and a man never cries. For this he earns well-being and respect.

At least I can shield Marcus from that view, but as we pass shopping malls, dog parks, drive-thrus, parking lots, I hear myself tell Marcus about the time a wounded blesbok gave his Pop-Pop three broken ribs, but he still made it for rounds with the lads.

"I'll take you hunting one day," I promise Marcus. But not here. There's hardly a squirrel to aim a slingshot at around here. We'll go on safari, and into the woods. We'll set up tents and build fires. We'll go out on the water in a boat and I'll teach him to point into the wave, not parallel. Too bad weather here is invisible; you start forgetting to factor it into your plans. Otherwise I could show Marcus that his old man could be the Noah of Anaheim. I'd take two of everything on my ark, except the gray-shanked doucs—I'd feed them to the dogs.

I pull into day care, and my pulse quickens: Donna is waiting on the curb for stragglers.

There is no shortage of pretty faces here, but *ag shame,* Donna's a stunner, the kind that turns heads. Mile-long legs and honey-colored hair, rumor has it that she's the bastard child of a chewed-up famous actor. You have to give it to our species. No matter how old and used up, we can still make the most delectable piece of ass.

Donna bounces up to my window. "Mr. Connor," she purrs in a singsong voice.

"Hello, Donna." Her name rolls off my tongue like mascarpone.

As I unstrap Marcus from his car seat, she launches into a winding explanation about her impending tript to Laos, how she told Julia, and how Julia told her that Laos was where Julia and I met, blah, blah. My mind arches back to Bokeo, the long trek with the Lahu men, the wild ginger and milkfruit meals and rice steamed in bamboo shoots; nightly

asphyxiation by insecticide in that cheap, godforsaken tent. It was the 157
only *Nat Geo* piece I ever did, but Donna dug it up in some archive, bless the internet, and is dying for an in-person account.

I strain my memory for impressive proper nouns but none appears. My brain cells are working too hard to stop from throwing my body down at her perfect feet. "Loads of insects," I say. "Wild pigs. Cobras."

"Cobras!" Her eyes widen like a Disney fawn, and really, I'm awestruck. I want to run a finger across those glossy lips.

"I've always dreamed of seeing an orangutan," she gushes, her eyes misty. I refrain from explaining that there are no orangutans in Indochina. She'll figure it out. Instead, I picture her in tiny shorts and hiking boots, strapped to a heavy backpack, and her million-dollar bust straining the seams of a tight yellow tank top.

"You'll have a lekker time. Bring plenty of repellant." I'm appalled by my paternal tone. I rack my mind for something to keep her talking. "I was thinking the other day. Can an attachment to stuffed animals get out of hand?"

Donna looks at my boy and ruffles his hair. Marcus grins his charming, gap-toothed smile. Good man.

"Does Marcus have a special friend we don't know about?" Donna asks. She turns to me. "I wouldn't worry, Mr. Connor. Who gave it to him? We were taught that many human-to-object attachments develop because of a strong bond to the gift giver."

Her hip pager buzzes.

"We'd better go in," she says. "You just have to tell me more about your adventures. And the girls want to hear about South Africa. We just *adore* your accent! We could listen to you talk all day." She bowls me over with those dazzling teeth and walks inside, hand-in-hand with Marcus.

I drive off in a daze. The monkey was first a gift to me, from a

158 conservation fund in Vietnam. My last paid project, over a year and a half ago. Bloody hell, that long? It's depressing. I gave it to my wife when I returned. She donated a hundred more bucks to the fund online. At my usual café haunt, instead of pitching articles or hunting for jobs, I fantasize about Donna. Donna in a yellow dress, Donna in leathers. Donna with her hair pulled back from full, flushed cheeks.

By the time I've satisfied myself with Donna in every which way, it's past noon and I'm so racked with guilt that I'm pushing ten over the speed limit to my wife's campus. The guilt edges up around me and erupts into a plan—lunch, a surprise, the two of us. The task now feels of paramount importance. If my wife decides to go home to eat, or if Larry drops by with the monkey, I'll have lost something, I don't know what, but I'll have lost.

My wife's office is in a building named after a rich patron who shares my surname. Perhaps, many generations ago, before his pops hit gold in the Wild West and mine hit the canteens in the Boer wars, our kin tilled the same Shropshire fields.

Today, a full-on battalion has blocked off Conner Hall and surrounded Baswell Fleck's statue. A hundred or so protesters bear signs, whistles, irritating noisemakers, and chant: WE REFUSE—TO REWARD YOUR HATE. WE REFUSE—TO REWARD YOUR HATE. WE REFUSE—

I join the queue of stalled cars waiting for campus security to part the hostile waters. One pimply string bean of a kid in a Patagonia shirt holds a misspelled sign with "Privalege" Sharpied in bubble letters. He catches me squinting and gives me the stink eye. Who do you think you are? The entitlement infuriates me, these Americans.

I turn my attention to a nearby bulletin board. Clubs, campaigns, promotional posters, advertisements are stapled onto the corkboard. *It's your time,* one ad says. *Turn a New Page Today.* LIFE STARTS NOW.

When I look back, a few protesters are glaring at me as if I have a swastika tattooed on my forehead. I roll down my window. "Have 159 you heard of manners, bru? Why don't you learn spelling before you organize—" A blaring horn drowns out my voice.

I pull my head back in the car and feel a rash rising around my neck. I reach for my phone instinctively, planning to call my wife and tell her to meet me on the main road. I stop. Would she come? If I had the monkey, I could have used it to lure her out. But I'm here empty-handed. It was meant to be a spontaneous lunch, like old times. I finger the keyboard of my phone, dawdling. What would I even say?

Up ahead, Campus Security talks to the protesters, points to me, talks again. A brick of a fellow in a fluorescent vest approaches my car. My stomach drops. If there's one thing I've learned from childhood, it's that the police, they can't be trusted. I roll down my window.

"Do we have a problem around here?" His tone says, *You're the problem.*

"I'm just trying to get through to Connor Hall," I say.

"That so? These folks say you were trying to provoke them."

"Look," I say. "Let's get one thing straight. This is your people's fight. I'm not even from this country. I'm a fokken immigrant! These youngsters are better off in class than blocking the lane."

Bloody hell. There I go, breaking the cardinal rule: Never contradict an officer. Another voice comes through, my wife's in my head. *This is America. You have rights. Defend yourself.* Whether she would deem my position *in the right* was a whole other matter.

"Let's change that tone, buddy," the officer starts.

I see a growing mob sneering my way, their faces a gallery of hostile masks. *Go home to your flush toilet and high-thread-count sheets. Keep living off the back of your oppressed wife, pretty boy.* Their chant begins to sound menacing. Menacing and personal. *We refuse to reward YOUR hate.* I spot a man with a notepad in their midst. It's a damn reporter, the buzzards. I'm out.

I throw up my hands, shake my head, and muttering, "You think your country is so ahead," I U-turn from the whole twisted scene, my head so hot that I almost run a red.

I bang the steering wheel and catch my breath. Moving here was a mistake. If we had moved to the farm, or even Durban, it wouldn't be like this. I would be on my turf; I would be useful; I wouldn't be hunted and stranded on this island of hate, hemmed by rules and formalities, shepherding my son to tea parties, competing with stuffed kiddie toys.

When I get home, I'll stick the monkey in the oven and turn on broil, watch him reduce to a cake of coal. I'll dunk him in a bucket of gasoline and take him to the roof, and I'll strap him to a pocket grenade, launch him to the stars and watch his pieces fall like a monkey comet over the L.A. skyline.

I would feel sorry for myself if I were sure I still loved my wife. How can I love someone who has lost all trace of her definition? She glides through space in a permanent daze, like an android maneuvering between assembly lines, because otherwise, she might miss a deadline or fitness class, a scheduled activity or catch-up call, coffee date, charity event with girlfriends. When I come close, her fog hardens into frosted glass, and who can speak his heart to a blurry pane? Who can apologize or compliment; who can explain that it *does* matter if she sits in the car while I ferry the boy around to day care, post office, groceries? I don't say, pay attention to me, because I'm not a monster, I know there are a million things she has to do to keep us in Target clothes and health foods in this giant shopping mall of a city, but. I'm not a chauffeur. I'm not a houseplant.

Sometimes, I think I love my wife more than I love myself. Sometimes, I no longer love myself. I can't even *see* myself. Not here, in this silicon wasteland, where everyone CrossFits and drinks probiotic fuel to make

themselves as strong as steel from the inside. I pass jogger after jogger
on the way home, and fuck me, I'm completely alone in this world. *We
refuse to reward your hate.* My wife's viperous eyes last night.

I try to remember a time when I've felt so unwanted.

✿   ✿   ✿

When I pull up to the house, Larry is outside, trimming the hedge
that separates our properties. "Your crabgrass is growing," he calls
cheerfully.

Like I don't have eyes. "Yebo," I say, and cut across his lawn. "My
son dropped his toy in your yard." I point to the area under my bedroom
window.

He sets down his hedge trimmers. "Come over and find it." He
motions for me to follow him through the front door.

I follow him in. The bright living room is crammed with wicker
furniture. I avert my eyes, afraid of what I might find. I see one of his
dolls in the corner. Larry catches my gaze but refrains from passing
comment.

He slides open the screen door to the backyard, and I follow him
around the side of his house. The monkey has fallen between the fence
and greenery. I go into the shrubs and fish it out. Its fur is matted and
a little damp, and the head is smudged with dirt.

"Can I see that?" he says. He brushes tanbark from the monkey's
twiggy legs. "Impressive craftsmanship."

"It's a douc langur monkey," I tell him. "Less than five hundred of
them left now, so they say."

Larry whistles and shakes his head. "Such a pity. Ever seen a real
one?"

I shake my head, no. Donna might. I never did, though in those jungle
nights, who knows, one might have made a cameo in my twitchy sleep.

162   We go back inside, and this time, I look at Larry's bachelor pad more closely. Mature bonsai trees line the window ledges, and one wall is covered with framed photos, some of a younger, freckled Larry, back when his mottled pink dome of a head was covered with sandy hair.

I spot a doll sitting behind a computer, her hands frozen over the keyboard. Buxom and brunette in a ribbed blue sweater, she looks strangely studious in her glasses. I'm grateful not to have Marcus tagging along on this mission. On the kitchen island is a wigless silicon head, surrounded by an assortment of tools and tubes.

"What are you working on there?" I ask.

"I'm learning to fix them myself," he explains. "Very breakable around the lips. You'd think they would be less hassle than a real woman." He smiles sheepishly.

At least he can tell the difference.

"Marguerite is the one at the desk. Workaholic, that one." Larry says.

"I gotta ask, Larry," I say. "You're a decent guy, nice place. Why the dolls?"

His eyes dart around the room, as if his ladies will chime in and rescue him. He shrugs. "Real women are cruel."

I think of my wife, provoking me nightly with her monkey prop, her *just-you-dare* look as I held the imposter over Larry's hedges. The kind of stare a small animal might give to a larger one for stealing her hard-earned kill.

"You're not wrong about that."

It is a way to live, I suppose. Minding his garden, minding his business. His dolls won't belittle him, won't punish him for failing to adapt.

A strong bond to the gift giver. I think back to Laos and those long-ago jungle days, when the world felt elemental. The natural order was simpler then; it made sense. Now the hierarchies were all confused.

"Do me one more favor," I tell Larry. "Let me borrow your hedge cutters." And swinging the filthy monkey by the tail with one hand, I go out the front door. On Larry's immaculate lawn, I toss the monkey on the ground and pin it with my foot. I pick up the trimmers. I grasp the handles, one in each hand, and with a mighty slice, I cut off his tail. It separates easily. So I sever each paw, one by one. The pieces fall on the grass like black petals.

Larry tenses behind me. "Is your son going to be happy about this?"

I cram the edge of the shears into the monkey's back seam, and I snip, from the white rump to the back of its head, until the fabric splits open and cotton stuffing cauliflowers onto the lawn. "He won't mind," I grunt.

Clumps of white fluff drift into the street.

As I carve the matted pelt into strips, a pressure releases, like a fever breaking open. I keep cutting. There are some things a man must do, for himself and his family. ✂

Min Han is a consultant at the World Bank. "Bond to the Gift Giver" is her first fiction in print.

PIRATES AND COWBOYS

REBECCA RUKEYSER

There was something wrong with all of them. Paula was cruel; she knew everyone's problems and proclaimed them in her Queensland accent. Sammy was afflicted with a blank, senseless rage. Maureen had lost her faith in Jesus, and the trust of her family because of that. Hans was flat-out defective. Jimmy James was a criminal; he held a degree from the University of North-Eastern London that he'd bought in Bangkok.

And what was wrong with Katherine? Katherine was mainly just very sad. She had been sad enough that it had been a liability back in America—her progress at school, and then at work, suffered. But Katherine had always had a lot of affection for her sadness. It was what made her Katherine. She checked in on her sadness periodically, in the way people run their tongues over their teeth, or count newborns' fingers and toes—okay, all there.

Katherine wasn't beautiful, but her sadness condemned her in the same way that a frail, blue-eyed beauty condemned other people. It made other people ask after her.

But Katherine was finally fired from her data entry job. In a frenzy of efficiency, she applied for a job teaching children English at a *hagwon* in Pohang, South Korea. She woke up the next day to an interview phone call. And until she flew across the Pacific she was too excited to be sad.

But once she was in Pohang, her sorrow returned. The first time **165**
Paula and Katherine really spoke, Katherine was crying in the stairwell
outside of O'Brien's Pub.

"Hey," said Paula. "What's wrong with you?"

Katherine shook her head and blew her nose into a cocktail napkin.
"Why am I here?"

"You need to pull yourself together," said Paula. She handed
Katherine a pill. "Here. Take this. I got it from my ear, nose, and throat
doctor." Katherine thought Paula was terrifying—that accent, like a
rake on cement—so she took it. The pill was amphetamine.

Katherine chatted to everyone as long as they'd allow it. She kissed
the bartender until she was bored with kissing, and then she walked
away, crushing up the ice in her drink with her newly sharp teeth.

Paula had been right; Katherine had needed to pull herself together.
Paula wasn't terrifying. Paula was Australian, but that didn't mean she
was made of scorched red dirt and poisonous creatures.

Katherine looked over at Paula. Paula gestured, "What's up?" with
a nod of her chin. Did Katherine want more pills? Here were five, right
now. All she needed to get a prescription was to take a taxi deep into
the Pohang suburbs, walk into Dr. Kim's office and say, "I'm fat. I want
some pills to not be fat."

How could Katherine not want more amphetamine? Before that
night the teachers at O'Brien's had mostly ignored her. Sadness was a
comparatively uninteresting problem in Pohang—only Paula had ever
asked her what was wrong.

And besides, she was teaching children English. She had never taught
before and it was exhausting. Children responded not to sadness but
to word games, games of hangman, snack parties, and an unspooling
cassette tape that played songs like "Trot, Trot to Boston."

166   On her lunch hour, Katherine sat with Paula in the pharmacy adjoining Dr. Kim's office, waiting for her prescription to be filled. There was a humidifier puffing that smelled like ginseng. Katherine had bought a package of Vitamin C chews and promptly ate half of them. The chews had the right amount of yield, in the cold interior of the pharmacy, for her restless jaws.

"I started in on these diet pills because my ex-coworker was on them," said Paula. "She was American, too. She was a cunt, but you seem all right."

"I am all right!" Katherine clasped her hands, caught by the updraft of the amphetamine. "I'm all right!"

They walked through the cold day to the taxi stand. Had Katherine ever felt cold like this before? The twiggy branches burned themselves into the pale sky. Her ears thudded.

"There are a couple of tricks to these diet pills, " said Paula. "One. Start the week with a halfsie. Take a halfsie until you need to take a whole pill."

"Yes ma'am."

"Yes ma'am? Don't be so American. Two—" she held up another finger. "Don't tell Dr. Kim if you lose weight. If you don't tell him—did you ever meet Angela? She was completely nuts. She was cracked— Angela didn't tell him, and even though she weighed forty-five kilos, Dr. Kim kept giving her prescriptions."

Katherine had the dogged feeling that something very important was about to come into her life. She kept that feeling in the taxi, all during work, and through until she fell asleep.

There was nothing that Paula didn't know: who was fucking who, who worked at each *hagwon*, who had been in Korea the longest. When Paula spilled the best gossip, the darkest secrets, she held her head tilted in a three-quarters profile. Katherine thought she was magnificent.

Why would anyone come to teach in a provincial Korean city instead of Seoul or Busan? Only if they were running away from something. Sammy—whose rage was the reason that the door of the elevator outside of O'Brien's Pub was dented—had been a rugby player in Auckland before he was kicked off his team. Jimmy James had been a cat burglar back in London, and people were pretty sure that he had stolen the O'Brien's bartender's laptop. Maureen, who lost her love of God and the respect of her community back in Canada, tried to hold dinner parties for the other teachers but grew feeble around the time that grace was usually said. Hans mostly just muttered to himself in Afrikaans, but Paula had seen him wearing a traffic cone on his head and yelling "American beef"—"*Miguk gogi! Miguk gogi!*"—in the middle of the street.

Suddenly, Katherine and Paula were best friends. They drank instant coffee on Paula's balcony overlooking brown, unflooded rice paddies. They talked all night. Even when it was fully dark Katherine knew Paula was studying her. Katherine could see the glint of Paula's eyes as they moved. The whole night glittered with shards of white: Paula's eyes and the pale rush of an egret ascending from the rice paddies and the lights snapping on in the other high-rise buildings and on the tower cranes of buildings being constructed.

There it was again: the sensation that something was going to happen! It was a ticklish sensation, and Katherine laughed.

"I've figured you out," said Paula. "There's nothing really wrong with you. You're sunny."

That statement didn't seem right. But what did seem right—what seemed cozy, glowing—was being considered, having Paula speculate about who she might be. Paula had thought her over and concluded she was sunny.

168   Maybe it was true. Maybe she was sunny. That week a student charged at her with scissors, gashing her arm. When her boss took her to the doctor's office to get the wound closed with adhesive, she told him, "I think Joon-Sook has problems."

"Yes," said her boss. "His parents are dead."

Katherine felt for her sadness where it usually was, in a vertical column behind her lungs, but it wasn't there.

Paula understood people. If Sammy were to get on the diet pills, Paula said, well, Sammy would destroy Pohang brick by brick with his bare hands. The diet pills helped mend, they fused the hairline fractures that hurt you, but they couldn't repair someone completely shattered like Hans. Jimmy James didn't *need* the diet pills; he was already ice-cold.

At O'Brien's, well after four in the morning, Paula said, "I like Jimmy James. I like his style. He's a pirate."

"Is he?"

Jimmy James was tubby in what Katherine thought was an English sort of way, weight put on with pastry. He was playing poker at the round table in the corner of O'Brien's. He was wearing a stocking cap with a fuzzy tassel.

"He's absolutely a pirate. He's absolutely one."

Katherine and Paula left the bar and Hans was sitting by a deflated advertisement for a BBQ restaurant, eating a bag of pretzels.

"They didn't have pretzels in Korea even two years ago," he said.

Jimmy James ran after Katherine and Paula.

"Where you going?" he said. He gave Katherine a wink while he was giving Paula a hug. Katherine told her about this. Paula laughed, and said, "No, I'm not sleeping with him! Jimmy James is like my older brother. He's my *oppa*. He's also a pirate who gets blow jobs from Thai prossies."

Did he now? In the cab back to Paula's house Katherine wondered whether that fact would have made her sad before. Now the thought glided emotionlessly out of her head and over the rice paddies. Every time the cab accelerated above eighty an automated voice from the odometer squawked "80! 80!" This made Paula and Katherine laugh.

"Here's a new rule," said Paula, with the same glorious authority she had when she declared Jimmy James was a pirate, the kind of authority that made it obvious she had been good at playing House as a girl, "If you ever start cracking up on the diet pills I'm going to just yell at you: *80! 80! 80!* And you'll do the same for me."

This was a system Paula had developed in Cairns. People were either pirates or they were cowboys. You just knew. Pirates were ice-cold, cowboys were softer. Pirates were amoral, cowboys had a code of morality even if it was warped. If two pirates fucked, they'd maybe murder each other. If two cowboys fucked, it would be boring. The sweet spot was a pirate and a cowboy having sex, with a pirate, naturally, on top.

"You," Paula said, raising her coffee cup at Katherine, "are a cowboy."

"Because I'm American?"

"Not just." Paula was a pirate.

Paula had told her she was sunny, and it had become true. Katherine bounded down the stairs of her *hagwon* to get shrimp and banana chips for student snack parties. She took her students outside to play inventive games: dodgeball with vocabulary, freeze-tag that involved yelling sentences in the correct tense. Her students drew a picture on the whiteboard of a smiling girl and labeled it "Katie Teacher."

So maybe she was a cowboy. She could get boots.

Sammy, perpetually enraged, was a pirate. Hans, who sat down on the curb when he was tired and would not be moved, was a cowboy with a cowboy's wordless patience.

"But what about Maureen?" Katherine asked Paula while they were drinking sweet potato lattes on Saturday afternoon.

They had just seen Maureen. She was on her way to Skin Food. "I noticed my coworker's skin looked pearlescent," Maureen said. "She told me that she bought a special compact." She walked back toward them fifteen minutes later, and her face—under her eyes, on the top of her cheeks—reflected the light.

"Do you want to join us?" asked Paula.

"No," said Maureen. "I'm going to Daegu."

"Maureen," said Paula, "Maureen breaks the mold. Maureen is a *fairy*."

"A fairy?" Katherine said, "What's a fairy?"

"A fairy," said Paula, taking a sip of her sweet potato latte and then patting the foam off of her lip while she thought, "is a rare creature. She seems soft, like a cowboy, but is actually ice-cold. She's also completely unpredictable."

"But Maureen's *Canadian*."

Maureen, unpredictably, returned back from Daegu with her hair dyed platinum blond. She had been in the salon so long that, she said, her scalp had started to burn from the bleach.

"What did I say?" said Paula. "Ice-cold."

Katherine thought about this. There was a knot of tears in her upper chest, and it gave her the same pain that she got when she swallowed too much bread with too little water. It was unfair that Maureen got to be a fairy. It was unfair that Katherine had to be part of a dismal fraternity of cowboys that included puffy, distraught Hans. Hans, who got excited about pretzels.

On Friday night Paula invited Maureen along for a dinner of galbi. Maureen talked, in her pert, sad Christian way, while Katherine grimly clipped the pork with the meat scissors.

"Did you have a crucifix over your bed?" Paula asked, turning the pork with the tongs and fishing up the choice bits for Maureen.

"No," said Maureen. "I had a picture of a lamb."

"Did you now?" asked Paula.

Katherine chewed the inside of her mouth when she wasn't chewing the galbi. Paula never asked Katherine questions.

Paula didn't have a clue about Maureen. There was no mystery to Maureen. Maureen was from Toronto. In elementary school Maureen had probably liked horses. In high school Maureen probably had French tip nails and spotless white sneakers. There were millions of Maureens.

But Paula treated Maureen as if she were a real fairy.

That week, Katherine took a full diet pill on Tuesday. By Thursday, Katherine was taking one and a half. She pantomimed baseball with her students, running through grammar points erratically; she almost lost her footing over the squat toilet in the bathroom. She flipped through all of the textbooks on her lunch hour. Were there any lessons coming up about fairies, or pirates and cowboys? There were not. There were lessons on how to navigate the supermarket and the airport and public transportation, and lessons on cities, and holidays, and ecosystems.

At O'Brien's, Paula talked to Maureen and Katherine talked to Jimmy James. Jimmy James, it seemed, was in a pickle. He needed to buy a ticket to Beijing so he could come back to Korea on a clean tourist visa, but he didn't have a credit card. "I'll pay you in cash when I get back," he said, and Katherine wanted to do something reckless and so said yes. He kissed Katherine's neck, a kiss between friendly and lascivious and said, "You're a doll."

Hans lurched by. He opened his mouth but all that he said was an oatmeal of vowels that ended with a question mark. Then he sat down, pulled his beanie over his eyes and lay his head down on the table. Sammy threw a cue ball at the head of a Korean man who claimed he was a talk-show host in Japan.

"Where did Maureen go?" asked Katherine.

"She has to take a cab all the way back to her apartment in the suburbs," said Paula. "She has to be up tomorrow to pose for a picture. They're putting her face on a banner advertising education, now that she's blond."

"When does she have to get up?"

"Like 8 A.M. Not to worry, though—I gave her a diet pill."

"Don't give Sammy one," Katherine said. Sammy was screaming, "Liar!" at the talk-show host.

"Everyone here is cracking up," said Paula, grabbing Katherine's arm. "Let's go back to my apartment."

On Paula's balcony, all Paula wanted to talk about was Maureen.

"I can't figure her out," said Paula. "Did you know she had to wear something called a purity ring?"

Paula took Maureen to get a prescription for the diet pills. Maureen loved the pills: she walked up each flight in her nineteen-story high-rise every evening. When Katherine saw her on Friday night Maureen had a sheen in her eyes that matched the pearlescent sheen of her cheeks.

"Shiny like a fairy," said Paula.

It was true that Maureen was more fun to be around when she was taking the diet pills. She now came to dinner every Friday, and talked breathlessly about her childhood as Paula gazed on. Katherine thought about holding a piece of charcoal up to Maureen's hair and watching it whoosh into flame. She thought about clipping Maureen's arms with the meat scissors.

Instead she said, "So do you like sheep? If you had a picture of a lamb?"

Maureen focused her pearlescent eyes on the embers of the barbeque and said, "I don't even know if I like animals."

Katherine's students were studying ecosystems when she came to a conclusion that was so beautiful it made her pulse squeak. They were learning unhelpful vocabulary like "taiga" and "savanna" and watching videos that showed birch forests, cherry blossoms, and mangroves. They labeled maps—blue for arctic, red for tropical—with the ecosystems stretching in jolly, equitable bands around the globe.

She told Paula they needed to meet. They needed to have coffee.

"What *is* it?" Paula asked at the coffee shop. "You didn't hook up with Jimmy James, did you?"

"Paula," Katherine leaned over the table. "I've come up with something. So there are cowboys and fairies and pirates, right? But we need something else. We know what these people are, but how do they *break*? How do they crack?"

"Yes," Paula said. "We do need to know how they crack."

"Ecosystems!" said Katherine. "There's a sliding scale right? From Arctic down to tropical. Take Sammy: Sammy's okay one minute and then throwing soju bottles down from the roof the next. He's Arctic. He breaks like an ice floe. Hans, on the other hand, is in a permanent state of decay, like the tropics. He's always breaking down."

"Yes. Yes, yes." Paula said. She took a whiteboard marker out of her bag and started writing on her napkin. "Okay. Maureen is Arctic. I'm Arctic. Sammy's Arctic. Jimmy James is maybe subtropic—he's not totally moldy like Hans, but he's on his way. And you—" Paula fitted the marker back into its cap with her teeth and looked hard at Katherine. "You're temperate."

"I'm temperate?"

"That's a *good* thing. Look at all the ridiculousness around you."

174 The waitress brought them two more lattes. "There's nothing wrong with you. Do you want to be tropical like Hans?"

So that was it, Katherine thought, in time to the click of her eyelids blinking over her dry eyes. A cowboy had two preordained paths in this world: to be overgrown by one's own madness like Hans with the traffic cone on his head shouting *Miguk gogi! Miguk gogi!* or to be sunny and temperate.

Katherine wanted desperately to cry, to show Paula that she held reserves of deep and interesting sorrow that someone temperate could never have, but the knot of dry bread in her chest wouldn't budge.

The next day Paula, ice-cold and icier because she was now Arctic, sat at the table in O'Brien's and issued cruel declarations: the Scottish girls that were hooking up were only lesbians because they were both fat and ugly. Sammy was banned from O'Brien's for two weeks because the guy he threw a cue ball at actually was a talk-show host in Japan, so he stood in the street outside and drank soju out of warm bottles and yelled up at the closed and curtained O'Brien's window. Hans showed up drunker and drunker, until the pink that always rimmed his eyes spread underneath them like a rash. Maureen's blond hair drew in the men at O'Brien's like she was someone new.

Katherine took two pills. She tried to get as drunk as possible, but it was impossible to lose clarity with two pills in her. Katherine drank vodka, because it was Arctic, and then spiced rum, because it was a pirate's drink.

Katherine spent the next day vomiting up what tasted of molasses. She went back to sleep and when she woke up it was dark and she felt a lurch that seemed like the beginning of tears but instead was more vomit. That week, Katherine took two pills every day. The class periods leapt forward in games of hopscotch. She wrote elaborate scripts for

the students to perform: "A Funny Day in the Supermarket" and "How
Will Ji-Young Get to Coit Tower?" It was warm enough that the snack
parties involved popsicles. All her tests were thoroughly graded and
her desk was organized. Her boss praised her for being neat.

On their way to O'Brien's, Paula, Maureen, and Katherine stopped
in Family Mart for a pack of cigarettes. Paula said, "Maureen! It's you!"
and pointed to a collagen-enhancing fruit drink in a tiny pink bottle.
The only words that weren't in Korean said "Fairy's Skin." Paula placed
the bottle on the counter.

"Every once in a while, there will be a person who isn't a cowboy
and isn't a pirate. That's you, Maureen. You're a fairy. You flew away.
I think you must be an Arctic fairy—you put up with everything for so
long, a long Arctic winter, and then your spring came and you cracked
off like part of a glacier."

In O'Brien's, everyone was hunkered around the bar. Korean
immigration wouldn't let Jimmy James back in to the country. They
looked at his passport and saw he'd been coming in and out of the
country for years and they closed the doors. He'd have to wait at least
three months. He was back in Thailand.

"Rest in peace, Jimmy James," they said, and raised their glasses.
Sammy was back, seething in the corner.

"Jimmy James is dead!" Sammy said, and then started trying to
break all of the pool cues. The bartender took him out into the stairwell,
and everyone could hear Sammy's yells, and the diminishing squeaking
of his sneaker soles against the stairs.

Then O'Brien's was silent. Paula turned to Maureen and turned
to Katherine and said, "Well, this is boring. I think we should go back
to mine."

"My money. Jimmy James has my money," said Katherine, but

176 Paula and Maureen were already leaving.

Out on the street there was no sign of Sammy or the bartender. There was only the late Friday night crowd of Pohang University students and salarymen, moving slowly in groups with their ties undone.

As they walked down the hill to the main street, Paula said, "So like Jimmy James. He's a pirate. He's sailed away to Thailand on his ship. He's gone now. I'm sure he's fine; he's ice-cold."

They all climbed in the cab, but Katherine sat in the front. Katherine turned around to look at Paula, but she was talking with Maureen in a voice that was so low Katherine couldn't hear. She wanted to cry. She wanted to cry so Paula would reach forward and grab her shoulder and say "Hey, what's wrong?"

Katherine turned around fully in her seat.

"I don't understand, Paula. Maureen is a fairy because she left. Jimmy James is a pirate because he left. I don't understand. If pirates can just sail away willy-nilly and fairies can just fly away on their fairy wings, what's the difference?"

Maureen's pearlescent eyes were big and reflected the dashboard lights.

"It doesn't work, Paula. It doesn't fucking work. I don't understand— Hans wasn't there tonight. Did he ride away on his cowboy horse? Did he? Did he?"

There was a stoplight coming up, the red spilling all over the wet cement. Katherine jumped out of the cab and slammed the door, and ran across the road. She didn't have to wait long; there was another cab, another interior that smelled like air freshener and the soiled smell of wet spring in the subtropics.

Katherine took the cab back to the neighborhood near O'Brien's. It was the same as it had been twenty minutes before. There were the same students, the same groups of slow salarymen.

177

There was also Hans, seated on the steps leading up to a café. His legs were splayed. He'd opened several bags of shrimp chips and banana chips on the stairs next to him the way that Korean children displayed snacks for a snack party, each bag ripped along one seam. There was also an empty Suntory bottle next to him, without its cap.

"Hans," Katherine said. He ate some snacks, but didn't answer. "Hans."

Hans moved his head in the direction of her voice. His irises vibrated as he tried to focus. Katherine could see from the movement of his irises the fact that the world was shuttering for him, his vision going from single to double. He moved onto one buttock and then shifted back.

"Hi," he said finally. "I know you. You're Katherine. You're so nice."

Katherine set down her bag and walked up to him, so close that she could see the full contours of his shiny cheeks, bunched as his tried to focus. She reached out and grabbed them carefully, as if they might burst in her hands.

They didn't, and she squeezed harder. She held his red cheeks in two handfuls; she squeezed as hard as she could. He opened his mouth and she could feel a line of sinew move at his jaw, so she reached for his stomach and started squeezing that, making grabs as if she could pinch some of it off. Her teeth were gritted and she dug her fingers in. He was silent, but kept shifting back and forth, so she made her hands into fists.

Instead of punching, she just brought her hands down—thump, thump—on top on his head. She thought about picking up the Suntory bottle and breaking it over his head. She could snip at his arms with the glass. If anyone asked why she'd done it, she could say, "I'm sad." She could lie; she could say something like, "My parents are dead." Or she could say nothing, and let everyone marvel at the intricate depth of her problems.

But instead of picking up the bottle, Katherine just thumped Hans until he bleated and brought his hand up to block hers. She brought her fist down on his palm and let it rest. His fingers were smooth. Then she turned around, picked up her bag, and walked to the taxi stand.

Paula called her the next day.

"*80! 80! 80!*" she said to Katherine. "You cracked it."

Katherine laughed, because it was only partially true. She hadn't hit Hans with a bottle. She hadn't burnt Maureen's lovely blond frizz of hair. Katherine was temperate. She would never know what it was to really crack, and that was exactly what was wrong with her. &<

Rebecca Rukeyser is an instructor at Heinrich-Heine Universitat, Dusseldorf, and co-founder of the Berlin Writers' Workshop. Her work has appeared in Best American Nonrequired Reading *and in Issue No. 97.*

SIGNS

SALLIE TISDALE

My friend moved to Bavaria, so after a time I went to Bavaria. She lived in the center of Amberg, a walled medieval town where the March snow lay bright across the hills and the pearly sky hung like drapery. She had one more day before her spring vacation, and left me in her spacious apartment above a medical clinic.

I dozed in her sunlit living room and then walked without aim through the frigid town, with its winding alleys and narrow roads. Small-paned bay windows leaned into my path. Everyone else was full of purpose—all good boots and red cheeks and clouds of breath. Children slid down the sides of the ancient dry moat outside the walls, where suburban traffic flashed by on the ring road. I wandered past the tiny stores selling coffee and books and bread and medicine and candy, wandered for hours in the curving streets through small tunnels and under archways, the stones cold as wounds. Except for one courteous drunk calling out "Guten Morgen" every few steps as she stumbled home at four A.M., no one had a lot to say. Neither did my friend when she returned, withdrawn into the cool Bavarian silence.

At week's end, we joined a line of stoic passengers for the flight to Rome, waiting out on the tarmac in a blizzard, snow piling up on our heads and shoulders like frosting. A few hours later, we were unpacking in a tiny third-floor apartment in a bright orange building on Via Andrea

180 Doria, looking over the warm Italian twilight. The dome of St. Peter's balanced on the horizon like a misshapen moon. The sidewalks were jammed with pedestrians, couples pushing strollers and teens in amoebic mobs and businessmen with cell phones pressed to their ears, hurrying past. The streets stuttered and rumbled in streams of boxy little cars, bicycles, scooters, wailing ambulances and swaying trucks and the occasional horse carriage. A drift of colorful confetti piled up against one curb. Police leaned on their muscular cycles, waving at the traffic with the exhausted disinterest of sunbathers.

In Amberg, pairs of white-aproned clerks had murmured "Grüs Gott" whenever I entered a store, then stood silently together with hands folded, waiting for my order. In Rome, every bakery and bar was jammed, symphonic. I backed out of the delicatessen, my phrase-book Italian unable to bear the weight of the jostling, determined crowd. The Romans were eating up their days, slurping and complaining with every bite, their words laid over and over each other in sheets of sound, woven under horns and squealing brakes and radios. Voices rose into the clear air like incense, weaving through the rooftop gardens of spindly antennae and scenting the laundry that hung outside shuttered windows. I imagined the housewives hauling in their dry pillowcases, listening to the muttering choir while they slept.

With weeks to prepare, I'd packed badly, taken the wrong train out of Frankfurt, arrived late. I'd spent solid years lying to myself, making big plans, trying to turn my life around like an ocean liner. I was lonely and bruised, and had come to see my friend as though on my way to a big audition. By the time we left Germany, we were split like sheaves. Now we walked through Rome together, not talking, like strangers who happened to be going in the same direction. I couldn't bring myself to ask what was wrong.

And yet. We were in Rome. We did what you do in Rome, a laminated city. We bought panini and gelato and morning cappuccinos. We ducked into internet cafés where she updated her Facebook page and I read email, hunched into a little cubicle between Skype conversations in Farsi and Greek. We walked through tiny piazzas, past designer windows and scrawny women tottering along the fissured sidewalks in pinpoint heels. We window-shopped for paper, maps, linens, buttons, willow furniture and Catholic vestments of startling luxury.

The fragments of stair beside a sidewalk, the broken pilasters in an alleyway, a battered column against the dry sky—traces not of the old city, but of an old city built on an older one, on one older still. Freud used Rome as an image for the mind, a place "in which nothing once constructed had perished." One need merely look sideways to see the line of time; debris lies under every cornerstone, the slough of ages. We toured the Colosseum with hundreds of other tourists, leaning over the gargantuan bowl full of sun and shaken by trains. Its dump of suffering lay crumbling in the slow erosion of moss and acidic air, left to postcards and paperweights.

One day, we followed the long, slanted face of the wall surrounding Vatican City. The sooty bricks were pimpled by small black holes, as though for messages—or perhaps arrows, which are after all a kind of message. Sparrows crouched in them, watching the mob with black birdy eyes. The immense Basilica snapped with golden light, filled with people taking pictures of the Swiss Guards and the sparrows and each other. Here Nero burned the Christians like torches in the mild Italian dusk. The Egyptian obelisk in its center is one of the oldest things in Rome. Caligula stole it, and a long time after that, Pope Sixtus V ordered it moved into the Basilica. It weighs about 320 tons, and the solemn procession required 800 people, 150 horses and 46 cranes. Sixtus decreed that anyone who spoke during the raising would be executed. The ropes caught; the obelisk was about to fall, and suddenly

182 a sailor named Bresca shouted, *"Acqua alle funi!"* Water to the ropes! he cried, and saved it. The pillar rises like an arrow, straight and true, thousands of miles, thousands of years, from where it was made. Bresca was willing to die for his pope's desire, but Sixtus was grateful enough not to kill him. Glad for small favors.

We crossed the leviathan space and filed with a thousand others through the great doors into the church. My friend went one way and I the other, wordless still. The building is impossible, bedecked on every surface. Each cove garnished, every basin polished, no inch untouched: mural, bronze, mosaic, fresco, painting, marble, gold, porphyry inlay and gilded stucco, gilt, framing, detail on every surface, no matter how dim or high or hidden. It houses forty-five altars, countless sarcophagi, and relics of all kinds—bones, teeth, two shoulders, and quite a few heads, according to Palladio.

I hesitated just inside the door of the church, paralyzed by detail. Small waves of eager visitors broke around me. I turned to the right and found myself looking at the *Pietà*.

A half-dozen people stood by the guardrail in front of the reinforced glass, taking photographs of Mary and the explanatory plaque and the glass and each other. Layers of cloth flowed like waves around her feet. Her left hand opens. Does she give? Receive? Beckon? Her hand opens ceaselessly. In her lap, he is almost smiling, as though in a dream. Her right hand holds him beneath his right arm, the muscles slack in death, soft against her strong fingers. His hands fall, flaccid. She does not look at his face, perhaps not *at* him at all, only down. Drapery mounds up around her face, falls in pleats and folds off her shoulders and arms; she is covered in so much fabric it is as though she is the one being shrouded. From an oblique angle, I could see a stack of cheap office chairs and a portable clothes rack piled at Mary's side.

Eventually my friend and I joined the panting, cheerful line of

people climbing to the top of the dome, a little Noah's Ark of humanity 183
huffing and mumbling in a dozen languages along bent and narrow
ramps, then across the catwalk inside, where white air swam and the
winter light broke into vapor before it slowly sank to the bedecked floor.
We climbed tight, narrow stairs in a spiral to the top. People stepped out
of the doorway breathless from the climb, a ceaseless line of travelers
shoving against each other, giving way around the edge of the dome
like a slow-flooding river filled with debris.

Crowded against the rail, I took a photograph of my friend and she
took a photograph of me, twins with eyes lost behind sunglasses, hair
torn by the wind, and the whole of the city behind us, spread out as
in a cartoon map on every side—the shining river, the gray ruins, the
parks and villas pale under the cold golden sun, this city made from the
deep conspiracies of old men. The hills and grassy walks looked like
cemetery grounds, soft and meaningless, lapped by whistling corvus
birds. I could see the distant Palatine where the dictators had lived,
where Domitian built a palace. He had a fondness for cutting off other
people's hands, and now all that is left of his beautiful floors are a
few broken marble tiles. They endure and Domitian is dust and for a
moment I felt fierce and glad.

One morning we were up with the sun, heading briskly off to the
Vatican Museums. More than a hundred Japanese lined up in front of the
group tour door. When the frescoes of the Sistine were restored several
years ago, a Japanese television station bought the right to air live footage
of the work, and now thousands of Japanese come to Rome. As soon as
we were in the doors, my friend joined the crowds at the counter, getting
headphones for the audio tour. I headed off alone through a series of
galleries opening one into the next like Russian dolls folded inside one
another—halls of tapestries and murals and maps and Etruscan bowls
and vestments and medals, the ceilings wrought with *trompe l'oeil* and

184 the floor a turmoil of *piedra dura*. The rooms were splendid and deranged, and as I walked they piled layer upon layer until I floated just above the floor in a fever dream. Somehow I went the wrong way, down the wrong stairs, through a door that should by all rights have been locked, and found myself in the Sistine Chapel, alone. The magnificent room was so still that for a moment I thought I might really be dreaming, that the dream had come true, that Italy was an empty maze of marble built just for me. Entranced by the light and green of the wild world, Wallace Stevens spoke of giving birth to something never seen before, to the mystery being brought into the world: "So, in me, come flinging / Forms, flames, and the flakes of flame." For a timeless moment, the chapel was empty and on fire and all for me.

But the room filled quickly until the floor was a great scrum of people. Many held the audio up to their ears, heads craned painfully back as they first stared upward into the transfixing vault and then turned to see *The Last Judgment,* its beauties and torments. This is the room where the old men choose successors, the pope's own chapel. I was close enough to see protrusions in the wall—small holes and pipes. For whatever reason that suited them, the masters of all this, these old Vatican men, have cut holes in *The Last Judgment.*

The Japanese, in matching hats, stood in tight bundles listening intently to lectures on medieval depictions of Christian martyrs and angels. They were the only ones listening; other tour leaders waved their paltry flags in vain. Everyone was talking under the *Quiet* sign and taking pictures under the *No Photos* signs. The guards were calm, resigned. "No photo," they said again and again into the din, without effort, "No photo." People took photos of the guards. Tourists are as old as dirt in these parts. Even the Catacombs were carried off by the cartload and sold as souvenirs. I sat there a long time, listening to the immense waves that had brought me here, hissing in their slide back to the sea.

In front of the Pantheon and its perfect antique curve, a drunk **185** American woman sprawled on the cobblestones near the fountain. A crowd of high school boys stared at her bare thighs while they ate Big Macs. I went into the McDonald's to pee, inching down narrow, wrought-iron spiral stairs. A long line of restive, perfect teenage girls leaned on the wall, waiting for the single stall. They were blank sheets beckoning the pen of time. Such dumb power. On my way out, I caught a glimpse of my face in the glass doors, beside the golden arch. For a moment, I didn't recognize myself. *I look tired,* I thought; *old* was the word I wouldn't say.

That night I crawled into bed with my journal and a glass of some sticky liqueur, and wrote *I am a kind of ruin.* I felt like a palimpsest with nothing underneath. A membrane seemed to seal me from the glassy world. What I think of as my history sprouts up through memory, so new; the origin is buried, long ago reworked and quarried into something completely different. We were still pretending all was well, and in truth I didn't know if something is wrong, if it was only me, if perhaps my brain was simply fizzing like a loose wire in the rain. I couldn't remember if this trip was her idea or mine. Sometimes it seems so easy. Human life. Talking. Then I try to talk and ash appears. How many offhand comments and little mistakes have flowed by, unnoticed? How many friends have I already forgotten?

Just before dawn I was jolted awake from a damp dream by a huge explosion; the glass in the window was ringing from the noise. Thunder shook the city like a bomb in great shaking bursts of noise and air, phosphorus flashes of white light shooting through the room. It stopped as it had begun, all at once, extinguished at dawn into golden sky and crystal light.

We had tickets for the Villa Borghese, to see the strange, exhilarating collection tumbled together in a great house in the center of a park. The

186 security at the Borghese was tighter than the Vatican's; our reservations were limited to a specific hour. We had to arrive well in advance to be admitted, but we couldn't figure out how to get there, exactly. The day was exquisite; the endless strata of Rome beckoned like a loving hand. It would be wrong to think these layers are a kind of series, as though sensible; they are disordered as completely as the floor of an old forest. But on certain mornings, I can almost believe in a plan.

A few days before, I had seen my face in a window and written *I am a kind of ruin*, and that morning I came across a line about Rome written by Geoff Dyer: *I was well on the way to becoming a ruin myself.* Maybe it is something about our age and maybe it is something about Rome but the disappointment is the same. I couldn't even mourn without imitation. My face was scratched with fine lines that seemed to carry a message in a language I no longer recalled—a graffiti of outlaw words. What would it be like to be truly plain, I wondered? To be unwritten upon and bare? My real dream now is to be excavated, slowly pried out of the dirt, revealed. Dug out, exposed to light again. My empty rooms open to the sky. Between the cracks, the sweet grass will grow.

Finally, we guessed on a subway stop. There were signs to Villa Borghese in the station, signs taking us down a long, empty hall. Everyone else walked the other way, but we followed the signs, a long hike up escalators and down escalators and up a short flight of stairs. When we finally exited, we found ourselves alone on a little island of dirt, with a busy street on one side and a high fence on the other. There was an overflowing trashcan beside the station door, and there were no signs there, no signs at all. ✄

Sallie Tisdale's most recent book is Advice for Future Corpses *(Touchstone). Her essay "The Hinge" was published in Issue No. 109.*

DISCLOSURES | IF YOU ARE AWARE OF ANY SETTLING

MOLLY SPENCER

After a while a wooded lot
means someday you will pay
to have the trees cut down.

The water spout on the door of the fridge
is just one more thing
that will break. These windows

are original, meaning
warped and in need
of repair.

Is there traffic noise, is there
airport noise, has the basement
ever flooded. Could the kids

bike to school. Why
is there all this unusable space
in the entry. You are tired

of trying to guess the reasons
they chose laminate
over hardwood

and the age of the furnace.
You would say
early two-thousands.

All the years it will take
for your hand to find the hall
light in the dark.

How the roof keeps
the rain off until it doesn't.
And winter nights—

the kids quiet in their beds,
the sliced blue threading
through inevitable cracks—

how you'll settle in front of the fire
listening to its shift and fall,
staring into flames of your own making.

Molly Spencer's poetry has appeared in the Gettysburg Review, New England Review, *and* Copper Nickel, *among other publications, as well as in Issue No. 104. She is the recipient of the Poetry Society of America's 2018 Lucile Medwick Memorial Award.*

MACHINES

SUSAN STEINBERG

This is a story about context. About things being out of context. There's no closer read to do than that.

Starting with my brother being out of context. A night my brother is on a dare. It's a nightly thing, this kind of dare.

Get in a stranger's car, they say.

Or, Get in a stranger's car, they say, and drive.

Parts of my brother's brain, these days, don't connect with other parts of his brain. It has something to do with synapses, something to do with neurons.

Think of it as short-circuiting. Fried wiring.

Think fork in the socket. Blow dryer in the bathtub.

Or just think the pills he takes that are our mother's pills for something. They're in a drawer by our mother's side of the bed. Our mother has said to us both, more than once, Don't ever touch this drawer.

But my brother is getting into everything that isn't his. Like other people's cars, and now our mother's drawer that our mother specifically said not to touch.

The market is always open. The locals are the ones who shop there. We only shop there when we're desperate and it's late. When we're out of something absolutely essential.

190 The cars outside the market are often unlocked. Sometimes the cars are running. The locals make it too easy for my brother. He gets into the cars like he owns them. It's a whole big show, my brother getting into the cars. And his friends just laugh, all fucked up, across the street.

My brother will only drive a car away once. That night he'll be missing for hours, and my brother's friends will all pretend they aren't worried. They'll make it into a joke how they often do with things that make them feel.

He's probably in another state, they'll say.

He's probably picked up a girl, they'll say.

But they'll drive around looking, all night, for my brother.

The cop will drive around all night.

He'll tell me to wait at the boathouse.

In case he goes there, he'll say.

So I'll wait on the boathouse lawn for my brother who I know will never show up.

On all of the other nights, my brother just stays in the lot. The locals come out of the market, see my brother sitting in their cars. They tap on the windows. Some of them pound their fists. Some of them open the doors and try to reason with my brother.

But most just stand away from the car, too confused by my brother to do a thing.

And it doesn't matter what they do, besides. My brother won't get out of their cars. The owners have to call for help. And when the cop comes, my brother's friends, assholes that they are, run.

This time, the owner is a woman. She's standing by a wall, holding a bag of groceries. My brother is in the passenger's seat. The cop is standing by the driver's side.

Some nights, the cop has to approach the car slowly. He has to make sure my brother isn't wild. Some nights, he's too worked up. Some nights, he takes swings at the cop. One night, he broke a windshield.

Some nights, he says things that make no sense. Like the time he spoke a series of numbers. The cop was like, What was that.

Some nights, my brother is passed out cold on the seat. On these nights, the cop has to call for backup, then other cops stand there, radios hissing on their shirts.

On these nights, the cop says I should go home. They can take it from there, he says.

On this night, though, my brother is awake. He's looking at the cop through the window. He makes his fingers into a gun. He points his gun at the cop. He points it at the cop's gun.

I hadn't noticed, before this, the cop's gun. I'm sure the cop doesn't use it. Because he isn't a real cop, but a summer cop. He looks too young to be a real cop. He isn't a cop who shoots at things.

When the phone rings, nights, our mother ignores it. My brother and his friends have turned, this summer, our mother says, into trouble.

My brother is pushing it, our mother says.

He is treading, she says, on thin ice.

But my brother is just fucked up in the way that most of us are this summer. The difference is he's learned how not to care. Or he's learned how not to feel.

Blame our mother's pills or blame some skill not all of us have. But our mother has reached her limit. She's at her absolute edge.

So I'm the one who answers the phone each time it rings. I'm the one who helps the cop with my brother sitting in some stranger's car.

I've been spending time, alone, in our father's study. Our father's study smells like apple tobacco, which doesn't smell like apples.

I was once attracted to the picture of the apple on the bag. So I once

192 tried to eat pieces of tobacco when our father was putting it into his pipe.

Our father said, Go ahead.

He said, It won't hurt you.

The tobacco tasted like dirt.

Our father said, Go ahead.

He said, It won't kill you.

The woman who owns the car is a local. You can tell this by her car. And by what she's wearing. And how she's standing against the wall.

She says, Get him out.

The cop says, Calm down.

She says, I will not calm down.

She hugs her bag and looks at her car, at my brother sitting inside it. But looking at him like that won't break him down. He's been known to sit for a very long time. And the cop has been known to stand there, useless, for just as long.

The night before our father left, he grabbed our mother's wrist as she was walking through a room. To talk, he said, but our mother said she had nothing to say and tried to pull away from our father.

Our father seemed to forget where we were. Not physically. But more in terms of schedule.

He seemed to forget he was scheduled to leave us the following day. That he was leaving us to be with a woman. That we were in the process of adjusting to his leaving.

My brother's friends will find the car my brother took stuck in sand by the water. They'll find my brother inside the car, his head pressed to the wheel.

At first, it'll look to his friends like my brother is sleeping. They'll make some jokes like wake that lazy fucker up. And they'll go on like this, as they often do, for as long as they can.

The cop knocks on the window. He has one hand on his nightstick. 193
I'm scared, I admit, of what might happen. Bad things have happened,
and the cop, too, is likely scared.

My brother presses his face to the window.

He says, Call my fucking mother.

He says, Call my fucking sister.

We have your sister, the cop says.

He says, This is your sister right here.

The cop shakes his head and looks at me. He laughs and wants me
to laugh as well. He wants this to be our private joke. My fucked up
brother not seeing that I'm right here.

But the cop isn't even a real cop. So I'm not going to have a joke
with him.

Instead I tell him to get my brother out of the car. It's his job, I say,
to get my brother out. Or I'll call our father, I say.

The cop doesn't want me calling our father. Even the locals know
what our father is like.

Not that our father is even around. I mean now that he's gone. But
the cop doesn't know our lives.

The girl once dared me to steal from the market. The thing I stole
had to be longer than my arm.

It was a dumb dare. There weren't many things that long in the
market.

There was beef jerky nearly as long as my arm. And there were
watermelons nearly that long.

I walked the aisles and found a statue of something holy. It was a
statue of a person. I can't even tell you who it was. And I didn't know if it
was for sale. But I walked right out, carrying the statue like it was mine.

I, too, have looked in our mother's drawer. I've held the bottle of pills. I've shaken it. I've opened it and looked inside.

I've thought about taking the pills. And I'll take the pills in the near future. Just to see if they do the same things to me. Make my brain fire all wild. Make me some broken-down machine.

Most nights, I walk my brother back to the house. He often wants to stop somewhere to eat. The only place open, besides the market, is on the boardwalk.

Then it's terrible having to sit with my brother. Terrible how fast he eats.

How I have to say, Slow down.

I have to say, It's not going to run off your plate.

In our father's study, I sit in his leather chair. I put my feet up on the desk. I put my feet up on the other leather chair.

In my head, I tell our father's woman, Sit here.

In my head, I tell her, Do this.

I can't tell you what this is about.

It's something to do with power. I mean my lack of power.

There are ways I want to hurt her.

There are many ways, I now can admit.

I won't hurt you, I tell her, in my head.

Our mother was kicking our father's legs. It was pathetic how weak our mother was. How persistent our father was.

He said, Kids, go to your rooms.

But we were too old to send to our rooms. So we stood right there and waited for our mother to win.

My brother's friends will think my brother is sleeping in the car. But my brother's arms won't be how sleeping people often hold their arms.

They'll then have a decision to make. To take this seriously or not.

They'll decide to take this seriously.
They'll try to open the doors. But the doors will be locked. The windows will be up. So they'll bang on the windows. They'll push on the body of the car.

When our father brought me into his study, it meant I was in trouble.

Like when I stole the statue from the market. The cashier dragged me back inside. He called our father and stared me down. Our father was enraged. Not enraged at me, but at the cashier for calling when our father was working.

Then, later, at home, it was me he was enraged with. Then he yelled at me for stealing. He said stealing was for the poor. And did I want people thinking I was poor.

I walked in on them, and the woman saw me walk in.

I've told this story a thousand times. I've told it a million fucking times.

That I saw them and she saw me. That she didn't let go of our father. That she looked at me while touching him like what are you going to do.

Like he's not your father now.

She said something into our father's ear.

There was a lot happening in a little time.

And I knew one of us in that room was to blame. Not just for that moment, but for all the moments that happened before and all that would happen after.

My brother punches the windshield, and the woman drops her bag.

I can see what sad groceries she's bought. I can see she's a desperate woman, and she's moving, now, toward her car.

This isn't a good idea. The cop and I know what my brother is capable of. Bad things have happened many times. So the cop tells the woman to stay where she is. He'll take care of this, he says.

196   But the woman says she's done. She's fed up, she says, with this dumb game. She wants to go home, she says.

And I wonder for a second about her home, what's even there.

Our mother never pulled away from our father. It was my brother who disconnected them. He yanked them apart with a force that surprised us all.

Then he left the house and didn't come back for the night.

Our mother went to a guestroom and slammed the door, then opened the door, then slammed it.

Our father just stood there, staring at a wall. I felt sorry for him in that moment, and then I didn't. And I didn't for a very long time.

But I will in the future, when he loses it all. I mean the near future. And I mean it all.

There are nights when my brother's brain is firing correctly. On these nights, he's more like he used to be.

On these nights, my brother says the other nights, the rougher nights, will make for a good story. Like someday they'll be funny to us.

Like the night he thought he was stuck on a lawn.

Like the night he let the dog fall from the window.

But it wasn't a good story, as it turned out, my brother just being a lazy fucker on a lawn.

And it wasn't a good story, the dog with three legs bandaged up.

Then all the nights him acting up in strangers' cars.

Then the car he drove away in. The car stuck in the sand. My brother inside, his head to the wheel.

Then one of his friends smashing a window. One of them running to the boathouse. One of them calling for help.

The cop standing by the car that day won't say, Good story.

But my brother won't be dead that day. He'll just be passed out like a dumb bitch. Just passed out cold at the wheel.

One night, we were eating dinner, and our mother left the room.

Then she came back holding a shirt, and said, What's this.

Our father, not looking up, said, What's what.

And our mother said, This, and held the shirt high, and our father looked up and said, What.

Our mother said, This, and our father sighed and looked at me and said, It looks like a shirt, and ate.

Our mother stretched out the shirt, which was a woman's shirt, and said, Whose shirt is this, and our father said, Is it yours.

Our mother said, No it's not mine, and our father said to me, Is it yours, and I said, No.

So our father said to my brother, Is it yours, and my brother looked at his plate, and our father laughed and said, I guess we have a mystery on our hands.

And our mother said, I guess we have a mystery on *your* hands, and she threw the shirt at our father, and it made a painful-sounding smack, and it fell into his food, and our father looked at us, and the phone was ringing, and our mother, again, left the room.

Now my brother punches the windshield harder. He punches with the force that's needed to crack it. We know the force that's needed.

The cop is reaching for his radio. There's static, then the cop talking numbers into his shirt.

The woman is walking through the lot. She's walking straight to her car. Her face looks fierce, and this will be something. This will be a whole big show.

Our father had brought me into his study. He told me to sit. Neither of us talked at first.

I could hear sounds from another room. Music or dishes. It doesn't

198 matter.

What you saw, he said.

What you think you saw, he said.

And I remembered a dream I had the night before. In the dream, I was standing in a field. And I was able to see the back of my head, while seeing through the front of my head.

And remembering the dream wasn't unlike having the dream.

I mean I was part there, part not.

Our father looked at me too hard. The study smelled like tobacco. And it wasn't even good for you. I'm not sure why he ever let me eat it.

What you think you saw, he said.

He said, You didn't see.

Then he held out his hand to shake mine.

We were making some kind of deal.

You can't say a word, he said.

You need to swear, he said.

On your mother's life, he said.

As if he even believed in the power of swearing.

I was at the point where I almost believed.

I mean I wanted so much to believe.

So I swore on our mother's life.

So I swore on our father's life.

Because fuck them both for putting me there.

So I was going to hell.

I told our mother after she found the shirt.

How I pushed the woman into the sink.

How I held her there like what are you going to do.

I mean I thought our mother would want to know.

I mean everyone wanted to know.

But the way our mother was looking at me.

Like I'd become some brutal guy.

Like I was now that fucking guy.

By the time I get to the car that night, my brother will be gone. One of his friends will have walked him home.

It'll just be the cop standing by the car. And it won't be night but light already. The following day already.

We'll both look at the water.

I'll be tempted to talk about it.

Say something about how still it is.

Or something about how blue it is.

But the cop will say, He's going to kill himself.

He'll say, Is that what you want.

I'll say, Is that what you want.

He'll say, Is that what you want.

The statue was big, and it was heavy, and it must have been important.

I meant to take it all the way to the boathouse. I meant to hold it high above my head. I would hold it like the holy thing I knew it was standing in for.

And the girl would just die laughing. Everyone would just die. Because what a fucked up thing, of all the things, to steal.

But they would never know the feeling I had standing outside the market. The feeling of power that came from stealing.

Or it came from the thing I stole.

Or it came from feeling like part of a club.

It came from our father, and I mean *Our father, who.*

For a second it felt holy.

And in the next second, I was stopped.

And had I not been caught, it might have been something that

200 changed my life for good.

Now my brother is punching the windshield with both fists.

In another context, this could be funny, his arms just firing, wild.

In that other context, this could be one of those stories we tell for years.

But there's nothing funny, in this moment, about my brother.

And there's nothing funny about the cop.

There's nothing funny at all about this night like any fucking night.

No, there's something funny about the woman.

It's the way she's running to her car.

The way her shoes land hard on the ground.

And the insects crashing into her face.

And her poor windshield about to crack.

And the cop saying, Stop, like she's going to stop.

The cop saying, I said stop, and what.

I mean what's the cop even going to do.

Do you think he's going to chase her down.

Do you think he's going to shoot her. ✄

Susan Steinberg is the author of the story collections Hydroplane *and* The End of Free Love, *published by FC2, and* Spectacle *(Graywolf Press). Her novel,* Machine, *is forthcoming from Graywolf this year.*

COMMUNITY SUPPORT
FOR LITERATURE & THE ARTS

Alexander Book Company

Bird & Beckett Books & Records

The Booksmith

DIESEL, A Bookstore

Farrar, Straus, & Giroux

Green Apple Books

Humboldt Distillery

Pegasus Books

Point Reyes Books

A Public Space

Skylight Books

Tin House

University of Nevada Press

A Public Space brings readers remarkable new writing and original voices from around the world, three times a year.

Get 10% off a one-year subscription to the magazine with your exclusive link. Offer valid through June 1.   apublicspace.org/store/subscribe/zyzzyva

Join the **Bette Howland** revival. *Calm Sea and Prosperous Voyage* is the first title from **A Public Space Books**, and the first book in more than thirty years by the iconic writer, recipient of one of the first MacArthur Fellowships and nearly lost to history. Until A Public Space found her again.